STORYL|NES

YOUR MAP TO UNDERSTANDING THE BIBLE

ANDY CROFT and MIKE PILAVACHI

David C Cook
transforming lives together

Published by David C. Cook
4050 Lee Vance View
Colorado Springs, CO 80918 U.S.A.

David C. Cook Distribution Canada
55 Woodslee Avenue, Paris, Ontario, Canada N3L 3E5

David C. Cook U.K., Kingsway Communications
Eastbourne, East Sussex BN23 6NT, England

Survivor is an imprint of David C. Cook
Kingsway Communications Ltd.
info@survivor.co.uk

David C. Cook and the graphic circle C logo
are registered trademarks of Cook Communications Ministries.

All Scripture quotations, unless otherwise indicated, are taken from the *Holy
Bible, New International Version®. NIV®.* Copyright © 1973, 1978, 1984 by
International Bible Society. Used by permission of Zondervan. All rights reserved.
Scripture quotations marked MSG are taken from *THE MESSAGE.* Copyright
© by Eugene H. Peterson 1993, 1994, 1995, 1996, 2000, 2001, 2002. Used
by permission of NavPress Publishing Group. Scripture quotations marked
KJV are taken from the King James Version of the Bible. (Public Domain.)
The authors have added italics to Scripture quotations for emphasis.

LCCN 2009910648
ISBN 978-1-4347-6475-1
eISBN 978-1-4347-0037-7

© 2008 Andrew Croft and Michael Pilavachi
First edition published by Kingsway Communications in 2008
© Andrew Croft and Mike Pilavachi, ISBN 978-1-84291-384-0.

The Team: Richard Herkes, Melanie Larson, Amy
Kiechlin, Caitlyn York, Karen Athen
Cover Design: Sarah Schultz
Cover Image: Veer

Printed in the United States of America
Second Edition 2010

1 2 3 4 5 6 7 8 9 10

123009

Dedications

Andy: To Mum and Dad—slow to anger and rich in love.

Mike: To Nicky and Pippa Gumbel—thank you for showing me more of the grace, humility, compassion, and integrity of Jesus. It means more than you know.

Contents

Acknowledgments

A big fat thank you to all those who have helped us draw out some of the themes of the Bible: Richard Herkes, Steve Croft, Ali Martin, Avner Boskey, Jon White, Tim Hughes, Matt Redman, Derek Morphew, Beth Coulson, Frog and Amy Orr Ewing, Jason Fout, Anna Williams, Melanie Larson, and Bishop David Pytches. Your time, patience, encouragement, and correction have been invaluable. We couldn't have done it without you!

We'd also like to thank Richard and Diana for their "home away from home"—your salad dressing is a catalyst for deep thinking.

Finally, it wouldn't be right for this book to be published without the two of us openly admitting we nicked most of the stuff in it from other people. To all those people who have taught and changed the way we read Scripture, who have opened our eyes to things we never would have seen ourselves, we are deeply indebted. Please don't sue …

Introduction

This is a book about a Book.

It's about a Book that tells of the birth of the cosmos. A Book that describes everything from the earthy cries of grieving mothers to the mysteries of the human soul. A Book with potential to restore our hearts and guide our lives, a Book upon which entire nations have based their worldview. This Book has literally changed the course of history. It's a Book over which people have fought and because of which people have died.

This is a book about a Book that tells a story. A true story. God's story … our story. So why write another book about the Bible?

First, we need the money. (Just kidding. Sorta.)

And secondly, more seriously, we are worried. These days there seem to be lots of followers of the God of the Bible who don't know where to begin reading it, who don't understand what's in it, and who are intimidated by it. And truthfully we often struggle to read the Bible ourselves. But we have also discovered that abandoning this Book puts our lives in peril. We have discovered that the Bible is the Book of truth and the Book of life. It feeds us, it challenges us, it guides us, and it comforts us. But more than anything else, the Bible points us beyond itself to its author, God. To put it bluntly, it's very hard to get to know God without reading the Bible.

As we've dug deeper into the Bible, we've glimpsed and unearthed treasures that we had no idea were hidden there. We have discovered just a few of the wonders of the Bible, and like two excited children who have found a secret garden, we want to show everyone who'll come and look.

Both Mike and I (I'm Andy, and I'm the one typing— unfortunately Mike has a typing speed of around ten words per hour) have been realizing over the past year or so that the best way for us to get to grips with the whole Bible is to understand the whole story. As followers of Jesus this isn't always as easy as we'd expect. Church services, youth group meetings, and Bible studies usually focus on only a small section of the story. This is definitely important, and because the Bible is so rich, we need to do this. At the same time, it can mean we grow up as Christians without ever getting the big picture. We can sit through Sunday school for years, trot out the right answers, have a nice discussion about particular biblical charac- ters—and still not "get it." Going through the Bible one snapshot at a time is like watching a movie frame by frame. Sometimes we just need to press play and watch it from start to finish. Then when we do come back to watching the individual frames, we're much more likely to understand them because we "get" the big picture.

Here's a quick map of what to expect in this book: We want to give a brief yet full overview of the Bible from Genesis to Revelation. We could have done this in many different ways, but the way we've chosen is to "paint" the story. It may be that some people who picked up a copy of *Storylines* are more familiar with the outline of the Bible story than others. For those readers who are a little unsure about the story of Israel in the Old Testament (the call of Israel, the split of the kingdom, and the captivity and exile), as well as the life of Jesus and the events of the early church, you may find it helpful to begin by first reading "The Bible in 20 Pages," Appendix A at the back of the book. This gives a whistle-stop tour of the narrative of Scripture and it explores how the whole of the Bible is the love story of God calling us into relationship with himself.

For those who feel like they already have a sketch outline of the story, we want to start to shade in the many contrasting and complementing colors by telling the story again through the different windows of the great themes of the Bible. Some verses will be looked at more than once; this is deliberate as we attempt to look through these different windows. At the end of each chapter you'll find a paperchase. In case you aren't familiar with the word, a paperchase is a child's thing—a playful following of a trail to see where it goes. In this book our paperchase will be similar; some fun trail-following. We'll do this by giving a summary of some of the key scriptures for that particular storyline. You may find it helpful to sit and read through them yourself, following the trail that God shows you. We know we'll have missed loads of amazing insights and wouldn't want you to lose out—the Bible is our ultimate picture and authority. There will also be two or three questions that you may want to read and think about yourself, or you may enjoy chatting about them with your friends.

Although every storyline follows the story of the Bible, each is very different and unique. Yet as we discover them, we begin to see that the Bible isn't just a random collection of sixty-six books; it's a stunningly coherent whole with an amazing purpose and a transforming message. We'll search out Jesus—the focus of the Bible—and realize the extent to which his life forms the plot of the whole story. We'll examine the covenants of the Bible and see afresh God's commitment to us from beginning to end. We'll experience the presence of God and come to know the point of it all is that we can *be with* him. We'll wonder at the mighty plan of salvation forging itself from Genesis to Revelation, and we'll stand in awe as the kingdom of God is brought about on earth as it is in heaven. We'll taste some of the worship of the Bible and recognize that the Scriptures are one long journey into praising God. If we understand these great themes, then we understand the story of the Bible, and even more importantly we understand God in a way that we've never understood him before.

We invite you to grab your Bible and come on a journey of discovery with us: We promise it will be worth the effort. It's our prayer that at the end of this little book we will all love the Book and the God of the Book more than ever before....

Andy and Mike

1

The Jesus Storyline

Years ago, when I was in my teens and Mike was having his first midlife crisis, a series of very popular picture books came out. Perhaps you remember them: They were called *Where's Waldo?* The basic idea was you would look at a big picture that would tell a story; there'd be loads of characters in it and tons of stuff going on. Waldo (a little bloke in a red-and-white shirt) was hiding somewhere in the picture. Sometimes he'd be up a tree, sometimes under water, sometimes he'd be in a massive crowd, often he'd be peering out from behind a corner, and almost always he'd be hidden from plain view. The challenge was to find him hidden in the story the picture told.

Two thousand years ago Jesus said to a bunch of Pharisees, "Where's Waldo?" But he said it like this, "You diligently study the Scriptures because you think that by them you possess eternal life. These are the Scriptures that testify about me, yet you refuse to come to me to have life" (John 5:39–40). Jesus wasn't talking about the New Testament, because his biography hadn't been written yet, so he must have been talking about the Old Testament. But how could he have been? Everyone knows the Old Testament was about Israel and Moses, David, Abraham, Joshua, and others. Did Jesus

get this one wrong? Had he eaten a rotten fig for breakfast? Or …
have we all been missing something? Could it be possible that, like
Waldo in the picture books, Jesus appears hidden all over the Old
Testament?

You probably already know that Jesus is all over the Bible; in the
Old Testament he's concealed, in the New Testament he's revealed.
Finding Jesus in the Old Testament is not just a game, like finding
Waldo. It's more like a treasure hunt, and it brings the story of
God to life in a whole new way. Throughout the Old Testament we
see strong hints, images, and prophecies about Jesus. In the New
Testament those hints, images, and prophecies are unveiled; the
curtain is ripped apart, from top to bottom, to reveal the star of the
whole show. Let's go on a journey together to find Jesus in the crowd
of Old Testament heroes.

Noah

> *The* LORD *saw how great man's wickedness on the
> earth had become, and that every inclination of
> the thoughts of his heart was only evil all the time.
> The* LORD *was grieved that he had made man on
> the earth, and his heart was filled with pain. So
> the* LORD *said, "I will wipe mankind, whom I
> have created, from the face of the earth—men and
> animals, and creatures that move along the ground,
> and birds of the air—for I am grieved that I have
> made them." But Noah found favor in the eyes of the*
> LORD*. (Gen. 6:5–8)*

The human race was so messed up there was no way to straighten it out. God decided to bring a flood and wipe out every creature. There was just one problem. Noah.

Noah and God were friends, and Noah was a righteous man. To destroy every living creature would have meant the unjust of killing his friend. God longed to save Noah, and so he commanded him to build a massive ark. We've been to the Middle East, and in case you hadn't realized, it's a desert! Despite how stupid he looked, Noah obeyed God to the point of humiliation. But it meant that, when the rains hit, Noah was saved. What's more, his whole family came with him. Why was Noah's family saved? Were they righteous? No. Noah was the only righteous one around, but because they were attached to him, his family got to come along!

The first hero of the Old Testament is our first signpost to Jesus. The flood didn't solve the problem of humanity's wickedness. God's righteous judgment is still that humanity deserves to die in its wickedness and be cut off from him forever. However, God has found one totally righteous man, even more righteous than Noah. This righteous man obeyed God to the point of utter humiliation, dying on a cross. What's more, all the unrighteous people who attach themselves to him are saved. After the flood a rainbow was the sign of God's promises; today it is the cross. All who shelter in Jesus, the ark of salvation, are not wiped out but given eternal life. Sometimes when we read about the cross, it can seem mysterious—something that's difficult to get our heads around. Discovering things like this throughout the Old Testament on one level helps us to understand it better—the patterns of salvation often reoccur. But on another level it speaks of the wonder and increases the mystery. Thousands of years before the birth of Jesus, God was carefully laying out the foundations for his master plan …

Abraham and Isaac

Several chapters later in Genesis, we come across a strange scene. In Genesis 22 we find an old man holding a knife over the chest of a young boy he's about to sacrifice. Years ago God had promised the old man that he would have a son, and after an age of waiting, Isaac was born. The baby became a boy, and Abraham loved him dearly. It was at that point God said to Abraham, "Take your son, your only son, Isaac, whom you love, and go to the region of Moriah. Sacrifice him there as a burnt offering on one of the mountains I will tell you about" (Gen. 22:2).

How could God command someone to sacrifice his own son? And yet—"For God so loved the world that he gave his one and only Son …" (John 3:16). The words of John, describing God's giving of his beloved Son, deliberately echo those of Genesis 22:2. God asked no more of Abraham than God himself was willing to give. God gave up his only Son, whom he loved, completely out of choice and love for us.

The old man obeyed God: "Early the next morning Abraham got up and saddled his donkey" (Gen. 22:3). Father, son, and donkey headed to the region of Moriah. When Mike and I visited Israel, we were amazed to discover that the region of Moriah is where, hundreds of years after Abraham, Jerusalem was built! And so when we read about Jesus entering Jerusalem riding on a donkey, we're reading about another father, another son, and another donkey riding into exactly the same area Abraham had been told to head to. In little, subtle ways—ways that we wouldn't notice unless we looked for them—God is laying down hints in the Old Testament of the plans he has for his Son in the New Testament.

When Abraham and Isaac arrived, we read that the father placed the wood for the sacrifice on the back of his son: "Abraham took the wood for the burnt offering and placed it on his son Isaac, and he himself carried the fire and the knife" (Gen. 22:6). Isaac then carried the wood for his own sacrifice up a hill in the region of Moriah. Isn't this amazing? Centuries later,the Father placed the cross, the wood for the sacrifice, on the back of his Son. Jesus then carried the wood for his own sacrifice up a hill in the region of Moriah.

Upon reaching the top of the hill, Isaac said to Abraham, "The fire and wood are here … but where is the lamb for the burnt offering?" (Gen. 22: 7). "Abraham answered, 'God himself will provide the lamb for the burnt offering, my son'" (Gen. 22:8). Abraham then tied his son to the wood and was about to kill him when the Lord cried for him to stop. God told Abraham to sacrifice a ram he saw caught in a hedge. Rejoicing, Abraham took it and sacrificed it in the place of his son. "So Abraham called that place The LORD Will Provide. And to this day it is said, 'On the mountain of the LORD it will be provided'"(Gen. 22:14). Two thousand years later on a mountain in the region of Moriah, the Lord did provide. He provided not a ram but a lamb for the offering … the Lamb of God. He is "my Son, whom I love; with you I am well pleased" (Luke 3:22). This provision of Jesus for us was something God had planned and intended from the beginning, before any of us were born. The storyline of Jesus running through the life of Abraham and Isaac shows us that even before most of the people in the Old Testament had been born, God knew what was going to happen, and he knew what it was going to cost him. He knew what you were going to cost—and then he went ahead anyway.

Joseph

So we move on to Joseph. Jesus is everywhere in his story. God's plan from the beginning, revealed to Joseph in his dreams (Gen. 37), was that he would achieve a high status and bring blessing and salvation to many others through that ruling status. Jesus was born to rule. He was born to be King, and because of his kingship many would find salvation.

Joseph's brothers became jealous and did what many of us want to do with our siblings: They sold him into slavery. Joseph was sold to merchants for twenty pieces of silver. Years later Jesus was sold to the Jewish leaders for thirty pieces of silver. Just think—if only it had been the same price, it would have been a perfect parallel … what a shame … But wait! The Bible tells us that Joseph was sold for the going price of a slave in 1900 BC and Jesus for the going price of a slave in AD 30. The price had gone up, but God had accounted for inflation!

Joseph was eventually sold to Potiphar, a high official in Egypt, and soon became his right-hand man. Mrs. Potiphar tried to seduce Joseph. She was very subtle—"Come to bed with me!" she begged. "No way, José!" Joseph replied, and when Mrs. Potiphar came in one door, he ran out the other. Jesus was tempted in the desert by the Devil. The Devil offered him all the kingdoms of the world if only Jesus would bow down and worship him. In response to the Devil's seduction, Jesus said, "Get lost!" (or words to that effect). By not sleeping with Potiphar's wife, Joseph resisted abusing the power his master had given him; by not "getting into bed" with the Devil, Jesus refused to abuse the power God had given him.

Mrs. Potiphar accused Joseph of a crime he did not commit. He was unjustly sentenced and thrown into the deepest dungeon. Jesus, years later, was accused of crimes he did not commit and was unjustly sentenced. While Joseph was serving his sentence, two criminals came to join him. Years later, while Jesus was serving his sentence on the cross, two criminals joined him. You can read in Genesis 40 about how Joseph, through the interpretation of a dream, spoke words of life to one of those criminals. Joseph promised he would be saved, and the criminal was later released. You can also read in Luke 23 about how, as he was dying between two criminals, Jesus spoke words of life to one. Jesus promised he would be saved, and we can be sure that criminal is now with Jesus in paradise.

Joseph was eventually released from prison. From the lowest pits of jail, he became Pharaoh's prime minister, the highest position in Egypt. He named his second son Ephraim (meaning "fruitful") and said, "God has made me fruitful in the land of my suffering" (Gen. 41:52). Egypt was an alien land that was not his home. When God became man, he was born into an alien land that was not his home, and yet it was in this land of suffering that God made Jesus fruitful. He was raised up from the lowest point—death—and is now seated at the right hand of God.

Famine struck the whole area, and Joseph's brothers came to Egypt to buy food. They were reunited with Joseph, the brother they'd sold into a life of slavery. Instead of having them killed, Joseph forgave them, assuring them, "You intended to harm me, but God intended it for good to accomplish what is now being done, the saving of many lives" (Gen. 50:20). He went on to save the lives of all his brothers, of those who had sinned against him. He brought them from a place of famine and death to one of abundant life.

The Jewish religious leaders, Pilate, and the Roman soldiers—as our representatives—accomplished what they intended in harming Jesus to the point of death on the cross. Jesus, as he was dying, cried out, "Father, forgive them" (Luke 23:34). We, the human race, meant the death of Jesus for harm, but God meant it for good. He intended it to accomplish what is now being fulfilled, a passage from certain death to abundant life, the saving of many lives.

Isn't this incredible? Joseph was born to be a ruler, he was sold into slavery, he was severely tempted, he went through great suffering, he predicted the salvation of one he suffered with, he was raised up again by God, he forgave those who'd sinned against him, and he declared it had happened that many might be saved.

Jesus' storyline is central to the story of the Bible, and it runs like a bullet through the story of Joseph. This is more than just an amazing biblical parallel—it carries with it a message for us today. Ever felt insecure about God's love? Ever been a little unsure as to whether or not he'll bring about what he's promised? Ever messed it up and thought, "It's been one too many; God's probably going to quit on me this time"? We can draw deep confidence from the fact that God *planned* his death on the cross. The way that Joseph's life prophesies Jesus' shows in an incredible way that God always thought we were going to be worth it—his decision to come to earth wasn't a last-minute afterthought. John's gospel tells us that Jesus is from "the beginning," and Joseph's story backs that up—he is from the beginning, and he was always going to bring about the ending. This picture is yet another guarantee to our hearts of the love God has—and has always had—for us.

Moses

Hundreds of years later the descendants of Joseph and his brothers had undergone a population explosion. They were now the people of Israel and were being used and abused as slaves by the Egyptians.

God heard the cry of those he loved, now slaves to Pharaoh, and through Moses he set out to do something about it. We read that, at the start of Exodus (chapter 3), the Lord revealed himself to Moses and commanded him to go and save the Israelites. Before he went anywhere, Moses wanted to know who this burning bush of a God was: "Who shall I say has sent me?" he asked. God replied, "I am who I am. This is what you are to say to the Israelites: 'I AM has sent me to you'" (Ex. 3:14). God's name was "I AM."

Also, Moses was understandably a bit nervous about taking on Egypt single-handedly, and he asked God, "Who am I, that I should go?" This time God ignored his question. He didn't say "You're Moses, kung fu champion!" He just replied, "I will be with you" (Ex. 3:12). The only thing Moses needed to know on this account was that God had his back.

So God's rescue operation for a people who were suffering as slaves involved one man. The reason this one man was going to save anyone was because God was with him. Who was this God that was with him? I AM.

Hundreds of years later God again heard the cry of those he loved who were slaves to sin, and through Jesus he set out to do something about it. Moses had asked the God of the burning bush who he was. The Pharisees asked Jesus, "Who do you think you are?" (John 8:53). Amazingly Jesus said in response, "'Before Abraham was born, I am!' At this, they picked up stones to stone him ..." (8:58–59). Some of the Jews responded with outrage; they wanted to kill Jesus. Why? Because he was claiming to be God. When they asked him who he was, he told them he was I AM. The God I AM went with Moses to save a people; the God I AM came in person to save a world. One of Jesus' titles is Emmanuel. It means "God with us."

Moses confronted the evil powers of Egypt, defeated them—and Pharaoh released Israel. They started the hike out of Egypt, but before long Pharaoh changed his mind; he sent everything he had after them. If we pick up the trail in Exodus 14, we find Israel trapped. In front of them lay the Red Sea, and behind them the Egyptian army was closing in. They had no options. Then God told Moses to raise his staff out over the waves of the Red Sea. Moses obeyed, and the waters parted. Through Moses' actions a way to freedom and life opened up—Israel now had one option! They passed through the waters and passed from death to life.

In front of all of us lies death; in and around all of us is the evil of this age. Do we have any options? Miraculously God provided an option for all who are trapped. Jesus defeated the evil power of this age (Satan); he conquered sin and death. Through Jesus' actions a way to freedom and life has opened up. We now have one option! In following Jesus we can be saved. Like the Israelites following Moses, on our journey we, too, pass through water in our crossing from death to life: "I tell you the truth, no one can enter the kingdom of

God unless he is born of water and the Spirit" (John 3:5). Ours is the water of baptism.

Moses' and Israel's hike through the wilderness went on for years and years. Mike and I recently went hiking down the Grand Canyon. It lasted for hours rather than years. Still, when we walked through the Grand Canyon, it was baking hot and hard work. After an hour or so, Mike started to moan … "I'm thirsty, I want some water!" He's Greek, so he tends to exaggerate, and he started to whine, "This is the end, I'm going to die!" Throughout the hike down, Mike complained, moaned, and whined at me. First he wanted water. Then he wanted food. After he'd eaten five PowerBars, he wanted a different sort of food … and so it went …

Moses was in a similar situation in the desert with Israel. They moaned, they whined, they groaned, and they rebelled. If we pick up the story in Exodus 32, we read that the people of Israel had just built themselves another god! Despite all God's amazing miracles they still mutinied and wanted to worship gods of their own hands. When Moses discovered this, he exclaimed in horror, "You have committed a great sin. But now I will go up to the LORD; perhaps I can make atonement for your sin" (Ex. 32:30).

Earlier, God, knowing what the people of Israel were up to, said to Moses, "Leave me alone so that my anger may burn against them and that I may destroy them. Then I will make you into a great nation" (Ex. 32:10).

What an offer! God told Moses to get out of the way; he was going to destroy Israel and start again with Moses' own children. Moses had a chance to get rid of the nation that had been a pain in his backside ever since leaving Egypt, and to start his own dynasty!

There were moments when, had God appeared to me at the bottom of the Grand Canyon and offered to kill Mike, I would have replied, "Brilliant idea, Lord! In fact I'll help you!"

Moses didn't respond like that. He didn't ask for a machine gun. Instead, after seeing Israel's sin, he said this: "Oh, what a great sin these people have committed! They have made themselves gods of gold. But now, please forgive their sin—but if not, then blot me out of the book you have written" (Ex. 32:31–32).

Astonishing! Instead of offering to help God wipe out Israel, Moses asked to be wiped out in their place! God refused Moses' offer. He had another plan. Moses' offer was well meant, but he didn't realize he didn't have the right qualifications. God didn't blot Moses out for the sake of Israel's sin. He already had someone else in mind. About 1,400 years later it was the life of Jesus, not the life of Moses, that was blotted out to make up for sin.

Sometimes the Bible can seem a little disjointed—we can read one story and wonder if it's got anything at all to do with the one we were reading the week before. Jesus is the center and the heart of the Bible; again here we see how the life and actions of Moses point forward to who Jesus is and what he was coming to do.

[Note: Mike would like it to be known that he was not allowed to contribute to this section, and in fact disassociates himself from the accuracy of the illustration used above … I, however, insist it's true, and I've got the emotional scars to prove it.]

David

David was born in the small town of Bethlehem. Samuel the prophet declared he was chosen by God to be king of Israel. When

Samuel poured the oil onto David, God anointed him for this task.
Soon afterward David fought the great battle with Goliath. We
find the site of the battle in 1 Samuel 17. The people of Israel
were lined up against their archenemies, the Philistines. The huge
Philistine champion would daily shout to all the Israelite soldiers,
"C'mon then, if you think you're tough enough!" None of Israel's
soldiers thought they were tough enough, and no one would go
and fight Goliath. This went on for weeks until David the shepherd
boy arrived and volunteered. He went out alone to face the enemy
as the representative of his people, Israel. David won a great victory without using the weapons of the world—he refused to wear a
sword or armor. Instead he used a sling, the weapon of a shepherd
boy, and it was in this apparent weakness that he defeated Goliath.
David declared, "All those gathered here will know that it is not by
sword or spear that the LORD saves; for the battle is the LORD's ..."
(1 Sam. 17:47).

Jesus was born in the *same* small town of Bethlehem. At Jesus'
baptism John the Baptist declared that Jesus had been chosen by
God to be the Savior of the world, and the Holy Spirit was poured
out on him (Luke 3:22)—Jesus was spiritually anointed for his task.
Having been prepared in this way, Jesus faced the Enemy of the
human race, Satan. He entered the battlefield of the desert where
he encountered and withstood Satan for forty days. Three years
later he went alone to the cross as the representative of the whole
world. He won the victory over Satan without using the weapons
of the world. Instead Jesus, the Good Shepherd, won the victory in
the weakness of the cross; it was not to be by sword or spear that
the Lord would save but by laying down his life for the sheep.

David was anointed to be king of Israel. Jesus, the Christ (which means "the anointed one"), was called "The King of the Jews" at his crucifixion. Jesus was also called "the Son of David," and people expected the Messiah to be like David. Many expected a David-type military leader who would arrive to kick the Romans' heads in. Jesus was like David, but not in the ways that were expected.

Of all David's psalms, Psalm 23 is the most well known, but the psalm that comes immediately before it is an incredible prophecy about the death of Jesus. It is one of the so-called "messianic psalms" (because it points ahead to the Messiah), and it begins with "My God, my God, why have you forsaken me?" Jesus knew his Scriptures, and so when he cried these words on the cross, he knew he was quoting from Psalm 22. Before we go on to look at this psalm further, we suggest you put this book down, open your Bible, and read Psalm 22 for yourself. Where do you see Jesus in this psalm?

Now let's look together:

The psalm that begins with the words "My God, my God, why have you forsaken me?" continues with many other striking references to Jesus on the cross.

David says, "But I am a worm and not a man, scorned by men and despised by the people. All who see me mock me; they hurl insults, shaking their heads: 'He trusts in the LORD; let the LORD rescue him. Let him deliver him, since he delights in him'" (22:6–8). The cries of scorn heaped on Jesus by those present at the crucifixion are almost identical:

> *In the same way the chief priests, the teachers of the*
> *law and the elders mocked him. "He saved others,"*

they said, "but he can't save himself! He's the King of
Israel! Let him come down now from the cross and
we will believe in him. He trusts in God. Let God
rescue him now if he wants him, for he said, 'I am
the Son of God.'" (Matt. 27:41–43)

The psalm continues, "From my mother's womb you have been my God" (Ps. 22:10). If anyone could say those words with more integrity than David, it was the son of Mary. The psalmist goes on, "My strength is dried up like a potsherd, and my tongue sticks to the roof of my mouth; you lay me in the dust of death" (22:15). The phrase "my tongue sticks to the roof of my mouth" is simply another way of saying "I'm thirsty." Jesus said on the cross, "I am thirsty" (John 19:28).

The next verse is translated, "Dogs have surrounded me; a band of evil men has encircled me, they have pierced my hands and my feet" (Ps. 22:16). David wrote these words hundreds of years *before* the Roman punishment of crucifixion had even been invented....

He continues, "They divide my garments among them and cast lots for my clothing" (22:18). Luke tells us that at the scene of Jesus' crucifixion "… they divided up his clothes by casting lots" (Luke 23:34).

Psalm 22:22 says, "I will declare your name to my brothers; in the congregation I will praise you." The stunning thing about this verse is that the writer to the Hebrews in the New Testament tells us that Jesus said it too: "So Jesus is not ashamed to call them brothers. He says, 'I will declare your name to my brothers; in the presence of the congregation I will sing your praises'" (Heb. 2:11–12).

Perhaps most amazing of all, the psalm that started with the words that began Jesus' crucifixion—"My God, my God, why have you forsaken me?"—ends with these five words: "for he has done it" (Ps. 22:31). Only Jesus was able to put these five words into the first person: "It is finished" (John 19:30). For he has done it—it is finished.

How amazing that David, without knowing it, should have written these words for the "Son of David," his Lord, to speak on the cross a thousand years later!

We have listed just a few of the references to Jesus in the Old Testament. There are many others. We encourage you to go on a treasure hunt of your own! None of this is to say that the stories in the Old Testament don't have a power, force, and meaning of their own—they do very much! In this chapter, however, we are only interested in tracing the storyline of Jesus through the Old Testament. It's like going to an IMAX cinema and being given special 3–D goggles when you go in. Try watching the screen without the goggles, and the pictures are there—though slightly blurred. Once you've put on the 3–D goggles, there's suddenly a whole new, sharp, remarkable dimension that comes into view. We've just watched some events of the lives of only a few of the characters of the Old Testament—Noah, Abraham, Isaac, Joseph, Moses, and David—wearing our 3–D goggles; even with only this brief snapshot, some of what was concealed has been revealed. What we need to remember is that this isn't just a clever joining of dots to make neat parallels—this is rich and glorious truth. It's the plan of salvation for our lives laid out through the lives of the Old Testament heroes. It's part of the mystery and wonder of God that he was able to weave the story of Jesus into the lives of his most faithful followers in the Old Testament in such an incredible way. In the same way, he is weaving the story of Jesus into our lives and our individual stories.

The Messianic Prophecies

There are also over three hundred prophecies in the Old Testament that are fulfilled in the birth, life, death, and resurrection of Jesus. As we said at the beginning of this chapter, Jesus identified himself in the Old Testament when he said to the Pharisees, "You diligently study the Scriptures because you think that by them you possess eternal life. These are the Scriptures that testify about me, yet you refuse to come to me to have life" (John 5:39–40).

At the end of the chapter, we've listed tons of the messianic prophecies, and we hope you'll take the time to open your Bible and discover more of them. But for now, we'd like to look at one of the most significant passages, found in Isaiah 53. Before this chapter Isaiah has been talking about the plight of Israel, how they have turned from their God, worshipped idols, and broken his laws by acting unjustly toward one another. The book of Isaiah begins before the exile in Babylon and then continues during the exile. Isaiah begins to speak hope to a hopeless people. He declares that God has not given up on his people and describes the coming of an anointed one, a Messiah who will bring salvation to Israel. In chapter 53 this Messiah is described in detail. We again urge you, put down this book, open the Bible to Isaiah 53, and read it. Too much explanation of this chapter is unnecessary; it speaks clearly for itself.

In Isaiah 53:2 we notice that when God came to earth, he didn't look like Brad Pitt. We are also told the coming king would be "a man of sorrows, and familiar with suffering" (53:3). This is key, as many of the Jews were expecting a victorious and powerful leader. Verse 6 lays out the sin for which the servant of God would die, the sin of human beings choosing their own way instead of God's. This verse reminds us that the heart of sin is going astray, choosing to live independently from him; the choice made by Adam and Eve. Verse 7 speaks of the fact that when Jesus, the Lamb of God, was brought before his accusers, he did not defend himself. Jesus himself even quotes verse 12 at the Last Supper in Luke 22:37: "It is written: 'And he was numbered with the transgressors'; and I tell you that this must be fulfilled in me. Yes, what is written about me is reaching its fulfillment." Isaiah 53 was fulfilled hundreds of years later when Jesus, dying on the cross, "bore the sin of many, and made intercession for the transgressors" (53:12).

We began this chapter by saying that Jesus is concealed in the Old Testament and revealed in the New. The fact is that Jesus hasn't been concealed very well—we've looked at only a few examples, yet pictures and prophecies of Jesus are all over the place!

What does all this tell us? First, Jesus Christ is the central character of the whole Bible. He does not just appear in the last scene. The person of Jesus is, if you like, the glue that holds the whole Bible together. Secondly, this tells us that Jesus was not Plan B. His birth, life, death, and resurrection were written into the script from the very beginning. Our sin and rebellion did not take God by surprise, and Father, Son, and Holy Spirit did not need to have an emergency cabinet meeting in heaven to work out the rescue plan. Before creation began, God knew that he would have to become part of, and suffer with, his creation. (Take a look at Revelation 13:8.)

A wise couple counts the cost before deciding to have a baby. There is the possibility of several months of vomiting followed by hours of agony for one partner. Then years of sleepless nights for both, followed by the expenditure of ridiculous amounts of money on toys, school uniforms, etc. Then more sleepless nights as they wonder where the teenage offspring are at 2:00 a.m. and even more expenditure if they try and send them to college.

A couple who has counted the cost of all this, but who has decided to love deeply and with commitment, decides to pay the price. God counted the cost and decided to pay the price. From the beginning he said we were worth it. From the beginning he said you were worth it. The whole of the Bible, the Word of God, is a revelation of Jesus, the Word made flesh.

A few years ago a friend of ours proposed to his girlfriend. He went all out. The day before the proposal he went into the countryside and laid an elaborate trail of messages. It began with a note hidden in the branch of a tree. The note was a love letter but also directions and clues as to where the next note was. She soon found, under a rock, another love letter with a clue as to where the next was hidden. Then there was another, inside a bottle concealed by a hedge. This went on for hours until she came to the final love letter. With this love letter, buried in the earth, was a box. When she opened the box, she saw the engagement ring, and he was already kneeling. The fact that he had gone to such a huge effort and carefully laid this elaborate trail was all to show her just how much he desired and loved her. Most women will never forget their wedding day; this woman will never forget the day he proposed. It was spectacular. He planned it down to the last detail; he left the clues everywhere, and it meant the world to her.

In the same way, we, as the bride of Christ (and we know this can seem corny), should be rejoicing and know ourselves to be much loved because our God has laid the paper trail throughout the Old Testament. He has hidden the clues of his love and amazing salvation. It is our prayer that as you've read this chapter you have gone on a journey of discovery, not simply of Jesus, but of how deep God's love is for us—of how he loved you before you were even conceived.

Jesus Storyline Paperchase:

- John 5:39–40 (Jesus asks, "Where's Waldo?")

Pictures in the lives of the Old Testament characters
- Genesis 6–9 (Noah)
- Genesis 22 (Abraham and Isaac)
- Genesis 37–50 (Joseph)
- Exodus 3, 14, 32 (Moses)
- 1 Samuel 17; Psalm 22 (David)

Messianic prophecies
As we said before, there are over three hundred prophecies about Jesus in the Old Testament that are fulfilled in the New Testament. To help you get started discovering the Jesus storyline throughout Scripture, we've listed a few of them for you, and we pray that God will reveal wonderful things to you as you study!

1. The Messiah will be born in Bethlehem

Micah 5:2–5a

"But you, Bethlehem Ephrathah, though you are small among the clans of Judah, out of you will come for me one who will be ruler over Israel, whose origins are from of old, from ancient times." Therefore Israel will be abandoned until the time when she who is in labor gives birth and the rest of his brothers return to join the Israelites. He will stand and shepherd his flock in the strength of the LORD, in the majesty of the name of the LORD his God. And they will live securely, for then his greatness will reach to the ends of the earth. And he will be their peace.

2. He will be King

Isaiah 9:6–7

For to us a child is born, to us a son is given, and the government will be on his shoulders. And he will be called Wonderful Counselor, Mighty God, Everlasting Father, Prince of Peace. Of the increase of his government and peace there will be no end. He will reign on David's throne and over his kingdom, establishing and upholding it with justice and righteousness from that time on and forever. The zeal of the LORD Almighty will accomplish this.

Daniel 7:13–14

In my vision at night I looked, and there before me was one like a son of man, coming with the clouds of heaven. He approached the Ancient of Days and was led into his presence. He was given authority, glory and sovereign power; all peoples, nations and men of every language worshiped him. His dominion is an everlasting dominion that will not pass away, and his kingdom is one that will never be destroyed.

Zechariah 9:9

Rejoice greatly, O Daughter of Zion! Shout, Daughter of Jerusalem! See, your king comes to you, righteous and having salvation, gentle and riding on a donkey, on a colt, the foal of a donkey.

3. He will be a descendant of David/family lineage

2 Samuel 7:12–16

When your days are over and you rest with your fathers, I will raise up your offspring to succeed you, who will come from your own body, and I will establish his kingdom. He is the one who will build a house for my Name, and I will establish the throne of his kingdom forever. I will be his father, and he will be my son. When he does wrong, I will punish him with the rod of men, with floggings inflicted by men. But my love will never be taken away from him, as I took it away from Saul, whom I removed from before you. Your house and your kingdom shall endure forever before me; your throne shall be established forever.

Psalm 132:11

The LORD swore an oath to David, a sure oath that he will not revoke: "One of your own descendants I will place on your throne ... "

Jeremiah 23:5–6

"The days are coming," declares the LORD, "when I will raise up to David a righteous Branch, a King who will reign wisely and do what is just and right in the land. In his days Judah will be saved and Israel will live in safety. This is the name by which he will be called: The LORD Our Righteousness."

Jeremiah 33:15

In those days and at that time I will make a righteous Branch sprout from David's line; he will do what is just and right in the land.

Isaiah 11:1

A shoot will come up from the stump of Jesse; from his roots a Branch will bear fruit.

Numbers 24:17

I see him, but not now; I behold him, but not near. A star will come out of Jacob; a scepter will rise out of Israel. He will crush the foreheads of Moab, the skulls of all the sons of Sheth.

4. He will be born of a virgin

Isaiah 7:14

Therefore the Lord himself will give you a sign: The virgin will be with child and will give birth to a son, and will call him Immanuel.

5. He will be a priest

Zechariah 6:11–13

Take the silver and gold and make a crown, and set it on the head of the high priest, Joshua son of Jehozadak. Tell him this is what the LORD *Almighty says: "Here is the man whose name is the Branch, and he will branch out from his place and build the temple of the* LORD. *It is he who will build the temple of the* LORD, *and he will be clothed with majesty and will sit and rule on his throne. And he will be a priest on his throne. And there will be harmony between the two."*

Psalm 110:4

The LORD *has sworn and will not change his mind: "You are a priest forever, in the order of Melchizedek."*

6. He will be Lord

Psalm 110:1

The LORD *says to my* LORD: *"Sit at my right hand until I make your enemies a footstool for your feet."*

7. He will be God

Isaiah 9:6

For to us a child is born, to us a son is given, and the government will be on his shoulders. And he will be called Wonderful Counselor, Mighty God, Everlasting Father, Prince of Peace.

Jeremiah 23:6

This is the name by which he will be called: The LORD *Our Righteousness.*

8. He will bring salvation

Isaiah 49:6

He says: "It is too small a thing for you to be my servant to restore the tribes of Jacob and bring back those of Israel I have kept. I will also make you a light for the Gentiles, that you may bring my salvation to the ends of the earth."

Zechariah 9:9

Rejoice greatly, O Daughter of Zion! Shout, Daughter of Jerusalem! See, your king comes to you, righteous and having salvation, gentle and riding on a donkey, on a colt, the foal of a donkey.

9. He will atone for sins

Isaiah 53:4–6

Surely he took up our infirmities and carried our sorrows, yet we considered him stricken by God, smitten by him, and afflicted. But he was pierced for our transgressions, he was crushed for our iniquities; the punishment that brought us peace was upon him, and by his wounds we are healed. We all, like sheep, have gone astray, each of us has turned to his own way; and the LORD has laid on him the iniquity of us all.

Isaiah 53:7–8

He was oppressed and afflicted, yet he did not open his mouth; he was led like a lamb to the slaughter, and as a sheep before her shearers is silent, so he did not open his mouth. By oppression and judgment he was taken away. And who can speak of his

descendants? For he was cut off from the land of the living;
for the transgression of my people he was stricken.

Isaiah 53:10–12

Yet it was the LORD's will to crush him and cause him to suffer,
and though the LORD makes his life a guilt offering, he will see
his offspring and prolong his days, and the will of the LORD will
prosper in his hand. After the suffering of his soul, he will see
the light of life and be satisfied; by his knowledge my righteous
servant will justify many, and he will bear their iniquities.
Therefore I will give him a portion among the great, and he
will divide the spoils with the strong, because he poured out
his life unto death, and was numbered with the transgressors.
For he bore the sin of many, and made intercession for the
transgressors.

10. He will heal the sick/preach the good news

Isaiah 61:1 (and whole chapter)

The Spirit of the Sovereign LORD is on me, because the LORD
has anointed me to preach good news to the poor. He has sent
me to bind up the brokenhearted, to proclaim freedom for the
captives and release from darkness for the prisoners …

Isaiah 35:5–6

Then will the eyes of the blind be opened and the ears of the deaf
unstopped. Then will the lame leap like a deer, and the mute
tongue shout for joy. Water will gush forth in the wilderness
and streams in the desert.

11. He will teach in parables

Psalm 78:2

I will open my mouth in parables, I will utter hidden things, things from of old ...

12. He will be a light to the Gentiles

Isaiah 42:6

I will keep you and will make you to be a covenant for the people and a light for the Gentiles ...

Isaiah 49:6

I will also make you a light for the Gentiles, that you may bring my salvation to the ends of the earth.

13. He will enter Jerusalem riding a donkey

Zechariah 9:9

Rejoice greatly, O Daughter of Zion! Shout, Daughter of Jerusalem! See, your king comes to you, righteous and having salvation, gentle and riding on a donkey, on a colt, the foal of a donkey.

14. He will be rejected/mocked/suffer and die

Isaiah 53:1–3 (and verses 4–12)

Who has believed our message and to whom has the arm of the LORD been revealed? He grew up before him like a tender shoot, and like a root out of dry ground. He had no beauty or majesty to attract us to him, nothing in his appearance that we should desire him. He was despised and rejected by men, a man of sorrows, and familiar with suffering. Like one from whom men hide their faces he was despised, and we esteemed him not.

Psalm 118:22

The stone the builders rejected has become the capstone.

Psalm 22:7–8

All who see me mock me; they hurl insults, shaking their heads: "He trusts in the LORD; let the LORD rescue him. Let him deliver him, since he delights in him."

15. His enemies will pierce his hands and feet, divide his clothes among themselves, and cast dice for his garments; and he will be served by future generations

Psalm 22:16–18

Dogs have surrounded me; a band of evil men has encircled me, they have pierced my hands and my feet. I can count all my bones; people stare and gloat over me. They divide my garments among them and cast lots for my clothing.

Psalm 22:30

Posterity will serve him; future generations will be told about the Lord.

16. He will be betrayed by a friend

Psalm 41:9

Even my close friend, whom I trusted, he who shared my bread, has lifted up his heel against me.

17. He will be betrayed for thirty pieces of silver

Zechariah 11:12

I told them, "If you think it best, give me my pay; but if not, keep it." So they paid me thirty pieces of silver.

18. The thirty pieces of silver will be thrown to the potter.

Zechariah 11:13

And the LORD said to me, "Throw it to the potter"—the handsome price at which they priced me! So I took the thirty pieces of silver and threw them into the house of the LORD to the potter.

19. He will be beaten, mocked, and spat upon

Isaiah 50:6

I offered my back to those who beat me, my cheeks to those who pulled out my beard; I did not hide my face from mocking and spitting.

20. His bones will not be broken

Psalm 34:19–20

A righteous man may have many troubles, but the LORD delivers him from them all; he protects all his bones, not one of them will be broken.

21. His side will be pierced

Zechariah 12:10

And I will pour out on the house of David and the inhabitants of Jerusalem a spirit of grace and supplication. They will look on me, the one they have pierced, and they will mourn for him as one mourns for an only child, and grieve bitterly for him as one grieves for a firstborn son.

22. He will be raised from the dead

Isaiah 53:8–12

By oppression and judgment he was taken away. And who can speak of his descendants? For he was cut off from the land of the living; for the transgression of my people he was stricken. He was assigned a grave with the wicked, and with the rich in his death, though he had done no violence, nor was any deceit in his mouth. Yet it was the LORD's will to crush him and cause him to suffer, and though the LORD makes his life a guilt offering, he will see his offspring and prolong his days, and the will of the LORD will prosper in his hand. After the suffering of his soul, he will see the light of life and be satisfied; by his knowledge my righteous servant will justify many, and he will bear their iniquities. Therefore I will give him a portion among the great, and he will divide the spoils with the strong, because he poured out his life unto death, and was numbered with the transgressors. For he bore the sin of many, and made intercession for the transgressors.

Psalm 16:10

… because you will not abandon me to the grave, nor will you let your Holy One see decay.

Psalm 49:15

But God will redeem my life from the grave; he will surely take me to himself.

23. He will ascend to heaven

Psalm 68:18

When you ascended on high, you led captives in your train; you received gifts from men, even from the rebellious—that you, O LORD God, might dwell there.

Discussion Questions:

- Are you surprised at the extent to which the Old Testament points to Jesus? If so, why? If not, then why aren't you?
- What does this tell us about the way that the Old Testament links to the New Testament?
- What practical relevance does this knowledge—that Jesus' life was foretold in so many miraculous ways—have?

2

The Covenant Storyline

It all began in the garden of Eden. When Adam and Eve turned from God to a life of independence, they left his presence. The story of the Bible is the story of God pursuing the human race ever since. He pursues us out of a longing for relationship with us; he wants to be near us. But God knows what every good counselor knows: For a relationship to last, there has to be commitment.

Commitment sees you through the bad days. Commitment is what stops you running after the girl or guy next door when you've had a fight with your spouse. Commitment is foundational for a relationship involving love and vulnerability. A non-religious marriage guidance organization called Relate recently published a book on sexual intercourse. Mike bought this book in order to find out what his married friends were up to, and because the title surprised him: *The Relate Guide to Sex in Loving Relationships*. When he opened the book, there was another surprise. While many of the pages were devoted to techniques for pleasing your partner, even more pages were devoted to an amazing discovery that the Relate counselors had made: More people have good sex in the context of mutual commitment than in the context of a one-night stand. God understood the basic principle behind this at the beginning of time—he made human beings to crave intimacy rather than variety.

The theme of covenant is not about legal technicalities of interest only to lawyers; it's about the making of a contract that provides safe boundaries for a relationship of mutual love between God and his people. The obvious picture here is marriage. Two days before writing this, we were at the wedding of two of our friends. They had been through a most horrific year: David collapsed at his bachelor party, was rushed to hospital, and had to have major brain surgery. At one point they weren't sure if he would live. There were many tears and many setbacks to his recovery; the wedding, of course, had to be postponed. David and Caroline went through agonies during the slow recovery. By the time the wedding day arrived, the two of them were desperate to be married. They had decided that they would be committed to each other for life, for better and for worse, in sickness and in health. After Caroline and David had proclaimed their love for one another and sworn their wedding vows, they sat to sign the marriage register—the contract of their union. This, we can honestly say, struck no one present as a dry, legal technicality; it was an amazing and wonderful moment, the sealing of a commitment of love for the rest of their lives. As they signed the contract, the moment became even more touching as a young woman sang beautifully, "How deep the Father's love for us, how vast beyond all measure." The love of the Father for us is not fleeting or fanciful; it is deep and unchangeable.

Another contract that symbolizes commitment is that of adoption. To adopt a child in our society often requires years of form-filling, interviews, and the matching of the parents to the adopted child. At the best of times this is a very complicated and difficult process. Our friends David and Minu adopted a baby girl from India. This was an incredibly painful, drawn-out, and expensive process. At the end of masses of interviews, checks, and forms filled, it was agreed that they could sign the papers. They committed themselves to be Ellie's mom and dad, to look after her, protect her, and love her for the rest of their lives. The adoption papers may have been signed with pen and ink, but even more than that they were signed with love. Two years later Ellie is the apple of their eye, and she is growing up to be a girl who is secure in the knowledge of her parents' love for her. Their commitment to her is unwavering.

A covenant, then, is not something dry, legal, and boring. It is a deep and powerful agreement that enables a loving relationship to flourish!

The Old Testament (the word *testament* means "covenant") gives us two key pictures of the covenant God made with Israel: the peace treaty and the marriage.

The Peace Treaty

Picking up the storyline of covenant through Scripture, the peace treaty is the first picture we come to. In ancient times peace treaties would often be made between a conquering king and the people he'd conquered. The initiator of a peace treaty would always be the conquering king. He would lay down the terms for peace. The three parts of the peace-treaty covenant would be the benefits to the conquered people, the obligations they would have, and the penalty clause they would pay if they did not meet the obligations. The benefits would be that the conquered people would get the protection and provision of the king. The obligations would be that they had to pay his taxes, obey his laws, and not swap him for another king. The penalty clause would be that if they chose not to obey his laws, he would withdraw his protection or punish them himself.

Contracts and covenants have not changed much today. A while ago Mike bought a car. He signed a contract with the bank. The benefit was that he got the car; he could drive through the countryside with his hair blowing in the wind. The obligation, Mike discovered, was that he had to pay the bank a very large amount of money each month for a very, very long time. The penalty clause: It was made clear to him that if he stopped paying the monthly payments, the bank would take back the car.

I, on the other hand, am less interested in cars and more interested in sports. At twenty-one I'm still young enough to dream of signing a contract with my favorite professional team. The benefits of this contract would be a disgustingly huge salary and my photo regularly on the back page of the newspapers (something Mike knows I would enjoy too much!). The obligations would be that I would have to train every day, eat lots of vegetables, be nice to the fans (even early in the morning, when I'm usually moody), and be loyal to the club. The penalty clauses of the contract would be—if I didn't train hard enough and lost form, or if I misbehaved—that I would be sold to a rubbish team and have the humiliation of playing in the bottom division. Something, I'm afraid, that Mike would consider to be perfect justice.

In the Old Testament the peace treaty was signed in a bizarre way. They would take an animal, cut it into pieces, and place the pieces between the conquering king and those he'd conquered. The king would then walk through the pieces toward his new people, representing the signing of the new contract. In Genesis 12, God appeared to Abram (Abraham before God changed his name) and immediately made a covenant with him. Abram's side of the covenant was to leave his country, his people—including his relatives—and go to a strange land that God would show him. God's part of the bargain was to make Abram into a great nation, bless him, and make him a blessing. He announced he would bless those who blessed Abram and curse those who cursed him. Through Abram all the nations of the earth would be blessed. Quite a spectacular agreement between two strangers! For some reason this wandering nomad chose to trust this deity he had never met before: "Abram believed the LORD, and he credited it to him as righteousness" (Gen. 15:6).

In Genesis 15 the covenant was sealed using the traditional symbolism of the time. God passed through animal pieces toward his new people—just as a conqueror would have sealed a covenant by passing through animal pieces toward his new subject.

Hundreds of years later God was faithful to his covenant when Abraham's descendants found themselves slaves to the Egyptians. Coming to Moses, he said, "I am the God of your father, the God of Abraham, the God of Isaac and the God of Jacob" (Ex. 3:6). Through Moses he commanded Pharaoh to let his people go. Having saved his people from Egypt, God then renewed his covenant at Sinai when he gave Moses the Ten Commandments. The benefits for Israel after they became subjects of God were the protection he gave to them and the blessings of security, health, and harvests that he poured out on them. The obligations for Israel were that they had to obey his laws, they had to worship him, and they were not to swap him for any other gods. If they did not fulfill the obligations, the penalty clause would come into effect. This would mean that God would withdraw his protection and would stop providing for them.

So God made his covenant with Abraham. Hundreds of years later he renewed his covenant with Israel at Sinai. Then, again years later, he repeated his promises, this time to the king who was most faithful to him: David.

In 2 Samuel 7, God repeats his promises about the land and then says to David, "The LORD declares to you that the LORD himself will establish a house for you …" (v. 11). He then says that David will have a son who will be "the one who will build a house for my Name, and I will establish the throne of his kingdom forever. I will be his father, and he will be my son" (vv. 13–14).

On one level this is fulfilled in Solomon because Solomon built the temple, which was the house of God, but actually this promise had another, deeper meaning. The descendant whose throne he would establish forever was not Solomon, who died; it was Jesus.

Apart from the faithfulness of David and a few others, much of the story of Israel from Mount Sinai onward is the story of how they messed up their part of the agreement. Reading the books of Kings and Chronicles, there were a few leaders who stuck close to God's laws, but most wandered away. They exchanged the God who'd made everything for little gods they'd made themselves. Israel just couldn't fulfil the obligations they'd committed themselves to. God sent the prophets to call Israel back to him, to remind them of the covenant he had made with them and to challenge them to repent and be faithful. Israel and their leaders refused. As a result God withdrew his protection, the people of Israel were conquered, they lost the land, they lost Jerusalem, and they lost the temple. The covenant was not to be taken lightly, and after hundreds of years of second chances the penalty clause came into full effect. Israel went into exile.

The Marriage

At the start of this chapter, we talked about how the covenant theme captures the love affair that takes place between God and Israel. No picture illustrates this better than the covenant picture of marriage. This picture is not more or less important than the picture of the peace treaty; it is the same view from a different perspective, and in the Old Testament it is another layer of the same story. When God brought his people out of Egypt and gave them his law, he in effect married them. He declared, "I will take you as my own people, and I will be your God" (Ex. 6:7). This is the heart of the theme of covenant and the heart of God's relationship with the human race.

The Bible uses the imagery of marriage to reveal and emphasize God's incredible passion for his "bride." We've already seen how Israel was unfaithful to her side of the covenant. Nevertheless, God kept pursuing her; he reaffirmed his covenant with her—both with Moses and with David. In the years after David, when Israel went completely off the rails, God sent prophet after prophet, not just to instruct her to obey the law, but to declare his love for her and beseech her to come back to him. The very first law is to love God.

One such prophet was Hosea. The book of Hosea is about a prophetic action that illustrates prophetic words. God told Hosea to marry and love an adulterous woman, probably a prostitute, someone he knew from the outset would break his heart. This was to illustrate the marriage of faithful God to unfaithful Israel, and how, even though it broke his heart, God could not bring himself to give her up. Hosea followed God's commands and married Gomer. Despite being totally loved by Hosea, and even having children with him, Gomer betrayed him again and again. Because of her adultery Hosea stopped showing love to Gomer. This is a symbol of God sending Israel into exile.

Perhaps, if it had been up to Hosea, he would have stayed divorced. But God told him that he must again take Gomer as his wife, paying a dowry for her: "The LORD said to me, 'Go, show your love to your wife again, though she is loved by another and is an adulteress. Love her as the LORD loves the Israelites, though they turn to other gods …'" (Hos. 3:1). So Hosea paid a price to have Gomer as his wife again. This was to show that despite the betrayal of Israel and the depths of God's hurt he could not simply divorce her (send her into exile) and be done with it. He was too in love. He said, "I will show my love to the one I called 'Not my loved one.' I will say to those called 'Not my people,' 'You are my people'; and they will say, 'You are my God'" (Hos. 2:23). God declared through Hosea his determination to bring Israel back to the heart of covenant, to the place where they recognized him alone as their God and themselves as his people.

Ezekiel is another of the prophets who paints this picture of marriage. One of the most beautiful, haunting, and tragic passages in the whole Bible is Ezekiel 16. Here we see more clearly than anywhere else how Israel's sin and rebellion broke God's heart, as well as his covenant. God, speaking through Ezekiel, begins by telling of how he found Israel just after she had been born, abandoned in a field and lying in her own blood:

> *You were thrown out into the open field, for on the*
> *day you were born you were despised. Then I passed*
> *by and saw you kicking about in your blood, and*
> *as you lay there in your blood I said to you, "Live!"*
> *I made you grow like a plant of the field. You grew*
> *up and developed and became the most beautiful of*
> *jewels. Your breasts were formed and your hair grew,*
> *you who were naked and bare. Later I passed by,*
> *and when I looked at you and saw that you were old*
> *enough for love, I spread the corner of my garment*
> *over you and covered your nakedness. I gave you my*
> *solemn oath and entered into a covenant with you,*
> *declares the Sovereign LORD, and you became mine.*
> *(Ezek. 16:5–8)*

In beautiful, tender language, the Lord talks of how he loved Israel unconditionally, protected her as she grew up, covered her nakedness, and then made a solemn covenant of marriage with her. The next section talks about how Israel took the beauty that was a gift from him and all the gifts that he had bestowed on her and used them to prostitute herself before every passing idol. She even sacrificed her children—who were his gift—before these idols.

> *And you took your sons and daughters whom you*
> *bore to me and sacrificed them as food to the idols.*
> *Was your prostitution not enough? You slaughtered*
> *my children and sacrificed them to the idols. In all*
> *your detestable practices and your prostitution you*

did not remember the days of your youth, when you
were naked and bare, kicking about in your blood.
(Ezek. 16:20–22)

So the unbelievable picture we have here is of a God who found Israel filthy, wretched, and abandoned, rescued her, clothed her, and protected her. Then, when she was old enough for love, he covered her nakedness and in effect became her husband. He made her beautiful, giving her jewels and fine clothes. Then she used her beauty to prostitute herself in front of images that she had made. Not only that, but she even killed the children that he gave her, in order to please these non-gods.

Mike and I recently went to Israel. While we were there, we saw, near Jerusalem, the valley of desolation, one of the places where the people of Israel sacrificed their children before a false god called Molech. What did God do?

Imagine your best friend gets married. He loves her with all that he has, but he comes home one day and finds her having sex with another man. How totally heartbroken he would be! But instead of walking away, your friend chooses to forgive his wife and continue with the marriage, still loving her as much as he did before. He comes home a week later, and this time she's sleeping with somebody else! The months go by, and she sleeps with anyone and everyone; she does it publicly and without feeling any sense of shame. One day he comes home and finds to his utter horror that she has murdered their children to please another man. Your friend is beyond devastated; he is totally shattered and absolutely broken. He comes to you for advice. What do you say?

If we were God's counselor at this point, we would have said, "God, you've given it your best shot. She'll never change; she's had too many lovers. It's not just that she's broken your heart, she's completely humiliated you! You've done everything you can to save this marriage. Now, for your sake, walk away ... get out ... in fact, when you think about it—she's an adulterer and a murderer—don't have anything to do with her!" Some have issues with the God of the Old Testament because he got so angry. An honest question, having read this, is why didn't he get more angry?

God didn't have us as his counselor; he didn't walk away. Instead he established a new covenant, one that caused him even more pain.

Israel failed to fulfill their obligations, and the penalty clause was exile. Israel broke God's heart and broke their commitment to him. Exile was God finally letting them leave. Exile was a hugely painful experience for the people of Israel, yet in the midst of this, there came the powerful promises of God, giving fresh hope:

> *"The time is coming," declares the LORD, "when I will make a new covenant with the house of Israel and with the house of Judah. It will not be like the covenant I made with their forefathers when I took them by the hand to lead them out of Egypt, because they broke my covenant, though I was a husband to them," declares the LORD. "This is the covenant I will make ... I will put my law in their minds and write it on their hearts. I will be their God and they will be my people ... they will all know me, from the least of them to the greatest ... For I will forgive*

their wickedness and remember their sins no more."
(Jer. 31:31–34)

Amazingly God promised that he would make a new agreement, a new contract, a new covenant with his people. Significantly, he announced it would not be like the old covenant … what then was the new covenant going to look like?

The Will

If the old covenant was based on a peace treaty and the picture of marriage, and it didn't work because the people could never meet the obligations, what would be the basis of the new covenant? Would God take some of the obligations away to make it easier? Maybe under the new agreement the Ten Commandments would be swapped for the Ten Polite Suggestions? Maybe God would soften the penalty clause—perhaps only community service as a punishment?

Many of us have been Christians for years—we've read the Bible and heard the talks—yet we can still forget the amazing terms of the new covenant. In this covenant God did not water down the obligations, he did not abolish the penalty clause—he would cease to be holy and just if he did. He knew that whatever he did we would never be able to meet the obligations and so, when it came to the new covenant, God didn't make it with us, he made it with himself! Father and Son shook hands on the deal. The nature of this covenant is spelled out in the book of Hebrews:

Christ is the mediator of a new covenant, that those
who are called may receive the promised eternal

inheritance—now that he has died as a ransom to
set them free from the sins committed under the first
covenant. In the case of a will, it is necessary to prove
the death of the one who made it, because a will is
in force only when somebody has died; it never takes
effect while the one who made it is living. (Heb.
9:15–17)

The picture that the New Testament gives of this covenant is the picture of the will. The basis of the new covenant is the last will and testament of Jesus Christ.

What's so special about a will? We all know the picture: Rich uncle dies, and we all gather round for the reading of the will. The tension levels are running high. Who will get the Jag, and who'll get stuck with the garden furniture? The will is useless until the maker of the will dies. Jesus died on the cross. The scroll is opened, and we discover that the inheritance is ours! We get more than the Jag and the garden furniture; everything that belongs to Jesus is ours! Imagine waking up one morning and discovering your dad is Bill Gates. You are heir to the Microsoft empire. Your laptop will never crash again. What we have is so much more than that!

Praise be to the God and Father of our Lord Jesus
Christ, who has blessed us in the heavenly realms
with every spiritual blessing in Christ. For he chose
us in him before the creation of the world to be holy
and blameless in his sight. In love he predestined us
to be adopted as his sons through Jesus Christ, in

accordance with his pleasure and will—to the praise
of his glorious grace, which he has freely given us in
the One he loves. In him we have redemption through
his blood, the forgiveness of sins, in accordance with
the riches of God's grace that he lavished on us with
all wisdom and understanding. (Eph. 1:3–8)

It's all ours because of him. What do we have to do? All we have to do is receive. Jesus said that if you know the truth then the truth will set you free. This truth will set us free from insecurity. Too many of us can't help but behave like little children who don't really believe that Mommy and Daddy won't leave them or abandon them. God should have walked away many times. He kept coming back, and he refuses to take no for an answer. He "will never leave you nor forsake you" (Josh. 1:5). The old covenant had benefits, obligations, and penalty clauses. The new covenant is different. The picture of the will is so incredible because the person who inherits does nothing but receive. Jesus has fulfilled the obligations on the cross. There he also paid the penalty clause. All we have to do is receive the benefits. This is called grace!

I know what you're thinking: *It can't be this easy, there has to be a catch.* The amazing, spectacular, magnificent, incredible, awesome, unbelievable, glorious, good news of Christianity is that it is as simple, and as easy, as that. Our salvation is a free gift, but one that cost him everything. The problem was not Israel—it's not that the covenant would have worked any better if it had been made with people from Yorkshire. It was not a problem with the Jews as much as with humanity. Humanity couldn't fulfill the obligations. So God, out of his amazing love, made this covenant with himself. Jesus made the covenant with his Father on our behalf. As the theologian Karl Barth said, "In Christ, God has at last found the perfect covenant-keeping partner."

So how does this affect the way we live our lives? It must change everything. This should bring an end to all our wonderings—"Oh, I messed it up today, maybe I'm out of God's kingdom"; "Oh, I managed to have a quiet time today, now I'm back in!" We must decide to put our faith in the facts and no longer in our feelings. The fact is that there is nothing we can do that will make God love us more, and nothing we can do to make him love us less. To know this glorious truth is to be liberated from legalism and condemnation and to walk free as an heir of the King. His love is deep and constant—and it will never fail (that's why the Bible calls it "unfailing love").

Does this mean we can ignore God's commands and do what we like? No, we are to obey God, but our reason for obeying is not to earn anything (it's already all ours!)—it's as a response to his love and as an expression of our love for him. Jesus said, "If you love me, you will obey what I command" (John 14:15). If the foundations of a house are right, that house will stay up. This amazing truth is the foundation for everything else. The reason we can have such security is that God's love does not depend on us—it depends on him. The glorious truth is he loves you, because he loves you, because he loves you. Never again doubt his love. Never again doubt your salvation. Your name is in his will.

Covenant Storyline Paperchase:

Old Testament pictures

Peace treaty:

- Genesis 15 (covenant made with Abraham)
- Exodus 19 (covenant renewed with Moses and Israel at Sinai)
- 2 Samuel 7 (covenant renewed with David)
- 2 Kings 21–25 (the Lord decides to send Judah into exile)

Marriage:

- Exodus 6:7 (the Lord takes Israel as his own people)
- Hosea (image of Israel as an adulterous wife to her husband, God)
- Ezekiel 16 (allegory of God caring for Israel and her unfaithfulness)

Promises of a new covenant:

- Jeremiah 31:31–34
- Ezekiel 37:26–27

New Testament picture

The will:

- Hebrews 9:15–17 (Christ as the mediator of the will)
- Ephesians 1:3–8 (our inheritance as adopted children of God)

Discussion Questions:

- What is the place of commitment in today's society and what does it mean to you?
- Do you think God *needs* us to be in a relationship with him? Why or why not?
- Do you feel that the terms of the new covenant have sunk into your heart? If so, what are the effects of that? If not, what barriers in your life are keeping you from this understanding? What will be the result of truly understanding this covenant?

3

The Presence Storyline

Have you ever been to a church meeting or service and, while you've been singing the same songs with the usual people in the same building, suddenly there is something that's indefinably different? It may be that as the last chords of a song fade away, nobody moves. You can't even hear the usual coughs; the atmosphere is electric; there's a heaviness that you can almost feel … nobody wants the worship to end. What is going on? Quite probably God has manifested his presence—in other words it's as if he's just shown up. But this begs the question: Hasn't he been there all along? Isn't he everywhere?

Of course God is everywhere … always. The technical term for this is *omnipresent*. He didn't just light the fuse and walk away when he created the universe—it's God who, through Christ, sustains the universe every moment of its being. Colossians 1:17 reads, "He is before all things, and in him all things hold together." Also God is always present when his people come together to worship him. Jesus said, "Where two or three come together in my name, there am I with them" (Matt. 18:20). He never misses church whether he seems to be there or not. This is clearly the teaching of the Bible.

At the same time, we see that there are particular moments when God manifests his presence in order to bless, rebuke, empower, comfort, or speak in a particular way. The burning bush; the dedication of the temple; Isaiah's vision; the day of Pentecost; the vision of John in Revelation; and supremely in the person of Jesus ... these are just a few examples of the many times in the Bible that God appears in a particular way. So in the Bible we see God is everywhere, but that he also manifests himself at particular times and in particular places.

We also see that the presence of God "indwells," i.e., lives in the people of God. In the Old Testament, God's Spirit filled prophets, priests, and kings. From the day of Pentecost in Acts 2, the same Spirit is poured out on "all flesh." It is no longer exclusively for prophets, priests, and kings; rather, all who ask for it will receive.

There are three words we see all over the Bible: *presence, glory,* and *holy.* In this chapter we'll define these words and show how they are inseparable. This storyline is crucial for our understanding of the holiness of God and the depth of intimacy he wants to have with us. Still, we are getting ahead of ourselves; let's start tracing this golden storyline from its genesis, the garden of Eden ...

The Holy Presence of God

As we have already seen, God created Adam and Eve for fellowship with him; they spent time walking around the garden with God and talking to him face-to-face. After they disobeyed God, they were too ashamed to be in his presence because of their sin and hid in the garden. Humanity ran away and hid from the presence of God. How many of us, when we sin, want to go and sit with God straight away? Once Adam and Eve had been made to leave Eden, they realized what it was to be outside the presence of God. Looking around them, they no longer saw paradise; they saw parched, barren, desolate land, and, looking at each other, they saw their bodies age. What was different between the garden and the wasteland? Between the place of life and the place of death? Was it simply that Eden had better soil? No, the difference was that it was in Eden that God chose to manifest his presence. This was where he hung out, and where the presence of God is, there is life! Paradise had been lost; sin and death came into the world.

Years later God manifested his presence in the desert of Midian to a fugitive named Moses. Walking the sheep one day, Moses came across a bush that was a little different from all the other bushes. God appeared to him at the burning bush, and when Moses approached, God said, "Take off your sandals, for the place where you are standing is holy ground" (Ex. 3:5). In Eden, Adam and Eve could hang out with God and not worry about anything. After sin had come into the world, this was no longer the case. Moses, before approaching the Lord, was made to remove his sandals. God's presence now had to be approached with caution; removing the sandals was an attempt to remove anything that might be impure before drawing near to God's holiness. It's like going to your posh relatives' home. You've just been playing footy, are covered in mud, and on the way step in dog poo. You walk into their home, march over their beautiful white carpet, and kiss your aunt on both cheeks—she looks horrified! You think, "What's wrong with my kiss?" Then you realize she's looking beyond you. You glance down, and dog poo footprints are covering the carpet. At the burning bush Moses' sin was like dog poo on God's holy carpet. From the outset of this storyline we start to realize that the presence of God is not something we can play around with. God is someone to be feared and respected, and we're to come before him with awe and reverence.

God's Presence in the Tabernacle

God is holy and so has to be "set apart" from sin. At the same time, this holy God longed to dwell among his people. By giving Israel the law, God sought to make for himself a holy people. By setting up the tabernacle and placing strict regulations around it, he sought to live among his holy people. He wasn't fussy, but he was pure. The regulations are God saying to his people, "There's nothing I want more than to live with you, but you've got to make an effort because I am holy." The tabernacle was the place that the very presence of God himself—the holy and separate God—dwelt in the midst of his people. The word in Hebrew literally means "the place of divine dwelling." Another name for the tabernacle was the Tent of Meeting, and it became, in effect, God's address on earth. Exodus 40:34–35 gives a description of God moving into his new address: "Then the cloud covered the Tent of Meeting, and the glory of the LORD filled the tabernacle. Moses could not enter the Tent of Meeting because the cloud had settled upon it, and the glory of the LORD filled the tabernacle."

"Have them make a sanctuary for me, and I will dwell among them. Make this tabernacle and all its furnishings exactly like the pattern I will show you" (Ex. 25:8–9). It was no small thing for the absolute holy God to choose to live among unholy people. He gave them an instruction manual much more complicated than any you'd find at IKEA. The point was not that he was fussy about his furniture, but that God would live among his people on his own terms. The tabernacle had "zones" of increasing holiness: There was an outer court, a "holy place" and a "most holy place." It was in the most holy place, the Holy of Holies, that the presence of God rested, and this was separated from the rest of the tent by a thick veil.

It's difficult for us in the twenty-first century to understand the rituals that were carried out before going into the tent where God lived (let alone the actual room in the tent where his presence rested); many of them seem very odd! It's a bit like some of the bizarre rituals we go through today before going on a first date. We wash very carefully, we may get our hair straighteners out, we'll select just the right cologne and exactly the right outfit; it's only having looked in the mirror for the sixteenth time that we're ready (and that's just the guys—guys who use hair straighteners, you know who you are!). Most guys know that often by the third date, women are telling us what they want us to wear and smell like.

That's what it was always like for Israel's representatives (the priests) before any big date in the presence of God. Our girlfriends may say, "Make sure you wear Hugo Boss (not the other cheap ones), and wear your best shirt (the one without the stains)." The reason many of us do what we're told is partly because we're "under the thumb," but mainly because by making an effort we can sit in her presence at dinner, or on the sofa, with that extra bit of confidence. God told the priests the smell he wanted them to have, the special clothes they were to wear, and the equipment they were to use. There was unique oil that was to be used only on the priests, and unique incense that was to be burned only in the Holy of Holies; all the temple equipment had been made to an exact design and dedicated to the Lord. Out of total awe and reverence for the holy God, a huge effort was made when one was near to his presence.

But that's not all. Only one person per year, the high priest, was actually allowed into the Holy of Holies, into the presence of God. The day on which the high priest entered the presence of God was called the Day of Atonement. To *atone* is to make up for sin. The English word *atonement* is created by combining the words "at-one-ment." Not much of a surprise there, I suppose! So to atone is to make up for sin—and it's also to bring about a reunion, a oneness between us and God. Atonement was symbolized by sacrifice; the high priest would sacrifice animals for his own sins and then for those of the people. This was the one time of the year that anyone was allowed behind the veil that separated off the Holy of Holies, the room where God dwelt. One of the meanings of the word *holiness* is "separate." A holy day is separated, cut off, from other days; holy ground is separated from other ground. What is it that makes something holy? The answer in the Old Testament seems to be the presence of God. Holy days were those given over to God, and holy objects were those dedicated to God.

So God has been longing to be close to humanity. They hid from him when they sinned in Eden, and his holiness meant he couldn't stand their sin. At last with Israel, a people whom he specially chose and to whom he'd given instructions on how to be near him, God found a way to rebuild this intimate relationship. He said to Israel that if they followed these instructions, "I will walk among you and be your God" (Lev. 26:12). All this stuff about tabernacles and incense comes down to friendship and relationship. It comes down to the amazing tension that on the one hand we worship and serve a

God who is mighty, independent, and completely beyond our comprehension—and on the other he's the God who delights in us and wants to be close to us.

The Presence Is Everything

A story in 1 Samuel 4—6 tells us more about what it is to have and to lose the presence of God. The people of Israel were getting beaten up by the Philistines. So someone had a great idea to bring the ark of the covenant from the town called Shiloh, where it was being kept. It was the ark that symbolized the presence of God, and it was made to house the stone tablets of the Ten Commandments. It also contained the staff of Aaron (Moses' brother), which had miraculously blossomed, and a jar of the manna God had sent to feed Israel in the wilderness. It was the centerpiece of the Holy of Holies, and God dwelt above it. They figured that, by bringing the actual physical dwelling of God onto the battlefield with them, they couldn't lose.

The Philistines won the battle and captured the ark of God—the Israelites had made the mistake of using God's holy presence as a good-luck charm. When the pregnant wife of Phinehas (one of the two priests who looked after the ark) was told that her husband had been killed and that the ark of the covenant was in the hands of the Philistines, she, in her distress, began to give birth prematurely. As she was dying, she named her newborn son Ichabod (which means "no glory"), saying, "The glory has departed from Israel" (1 Sam. 4:21).

If the capture of the ark was a disaster for Israel, it was a total nightmare for the Philistines! They made the mistake of parking God's presence next to the image of their own god, Dagon. In the morning the statue of Dagon was in pieces on the floor, face down before the ark of God. Then the Philistines started growing tumors and dying. They realized that they were being judged in the presence of the God of Israel, and so they put the ark on a cart and hitched it to a cow. The cow of its own accord led the ark back into Israel.

From this story we learn the power of the presence of God. Sometimes we in the church can treat God's presence simply as a teddy bear, but he is an awesome, terrible, and holy God. It can be wonderful for those who are the people of God and who choose to honor his holiness. It can be terrible for those who are not the people of God or who choose to lead lives of rebellion against God. Mrs. Phinehas and the rest of Israel knew when God's glory had departed. The question is, in our rational, intellectual, sophisticated, twenty-first-century church, do we?

A famous evangelist used to pose the challenge, "If the Holy Spirit left your church, would anybody notice?" That is one of the big questions we, the church, have to answer in our day. The longing in people's hearts ought not to be for a church that is more slick, entertaining, or comfortable; we desperately need a church that is more filled with the powerful presence of God.

Later in the story of the Bible, we see that King David planned, and his son King Solomon built, a permanent temple for God. Until this point God's address had been the tabernacle constructed by Moses. The temple was built in the center of Jerusalem and, just like the tabernacle, was designed with zones of holiness. The Holy of Holies was the focus of the temple. The heart of Israel's worship was Jerusalem, the heart of Jerusalem was the temple, the heart of the temple was the Holy of Holies, and the heartbeat of the Holy of Holies was the manifest presence of God.

The Glory of the Presence

Another key story that helps us understand the significance and importance of the presence of God can be found in 2 Chronicles 5—7. It tells us of the completion and dedication of the temple. The ark is brought into the most holy place; the priests, the trumpeters, and the singers all praise God, singing: "'He is good; his love endures forever.' Then the temple of the LORD was filled with a cloud, and the priests could not perform their service because of the cloud, for the glory of the LORD filled the temple of God" (2 Chron. 5:13–14).

At this point Solomon got up and prayed a long prayer of dedication, at the end of which we read:

> *When Solomon finished praying, fire came down from heaven and consumed the burnt offering and the sacrifices, and the glory of the LORD filled the temple. The priests could not enter the temple of the LORD because the glory of the LORD filled it. When all the Israelites saw the fire coming down and the glory of the LORD above the temple, they knelt on the pavement with their faces to the ground, and they worshipped and gave thanks to the LORD, saying, "He is good; his love endures forever." (2 Chron. 7:1–3)*

What an amazing meeting! Have you ever wondered about the glory of God? The glory of God here is shown to be the manifest presence of God. If there's one thing that is explicit, it's that you KNOW when the glory of God arrives. Just as Phinehas's wife knew when the glory had departed from Israel, so the Israelites knew when the glory fell on the temple. It wasn't just an intellectual realization; it was unquestionably an experience.

Our friend Matt Redman wrote a song, the first verse of which says, "Lord, let your glory fall as on that ancient day, songs of enduring love and then your glory came. And as a sign to you that we would love the same, our hearts will sing that song, God let your glory come!"[1] He was talking about that ancient day, the day the glory of God fell on his temple. In this modern day we need to do more than just sing another Matt Redman song; we need to cry, to call out to God, for his glory to fall. We will only really do that when we realize that it is the presence of God that makes all the difference.

Created to Be in His Presence

These stories show us that to live in God's presence is what we were created for—remember Eden—and that God did everything to live among his people. Moses understood the necessity of living in the presence of God. In Exodus 33 he told God, "If your Presence does not go with us [Israel], do not send us up from here…. What else will distinguish me and your people from all the other people on the face of the earth?" (vv. 15–16). Moses had learned that to go even into the Promised Land (a land of plenty and prosperity) without the presence of God was a waste of time. It was God's presence that marked Israel as God's people. Christians today are not, generally, better looking, funnier, better dressed, or smarter than non-Christians. God's presence and God's presence alone distinguishes us. It was only God's presence that gave meaning to the tabernacle and then to the temple as the place of worship. It is all about his presence!

The Presence Is Lost

The prophetic book of Ezekiel is one of the wackiest in the Bible. We meet wheels within wheels, chariots of fire, and a man who spends 390 days lying on one side, in addition to shaving all his hair off in order to perform different crazy but symbolic acts with it. We can understand why Ezekiel might be thought to be one sandwich short of the full picnic. However, the book of Ezekiel is a key to a deeper understanding of the meaning of the glorious presence of our God.

Ezekiel received his visions while with the Israelites in exile in Babylon. In chapter 8, Ezekiel has a vision in which he's transported to the temple back in Jerusalem. In the temple he is shown four horrendous scenes. They show different scenes of the people of Israel worshipping idols, and they highlight how Israel is sinning on the very doorstep of God's house. The last and worst act Ezekiel is shown is in the inner court of the temple, just outside the sanctuary of God. Here there are twenty-five men, with their backs to the sanctuary, prostrating themselves and worshipping the sun. The seriousness, scale, and shame of this sin is huge. Imagine returning home to find not only that your wife or husband is committing adultery, but that, disgustingly, they've been having sex in the bed the two of you are meant to share. Israel's repeated sin penetrated even to the most sacred of places.

The holy God had longed to dwell with his people. Since their time in Egypt, Israel had been repeatedly turning away from God. He had sent them warning after warning, prophet after prophet, trying and trying to call his rebellious people back to him. The holy God, the God who kept himself separate from all that was unholy, had set aside the temple as his dwelling place. It is no coincidence that when describing Israel's sin Ezekiel repeatedly uses the phrase "to profane"—the opposite of "to make holy" (thirty-nine of the seventy-one appearances of the word *profane* in the Bible occur in Ezekiel).

It is often the holy name of God that is described as being profaned, and in one striking phrase God himself announces, "You have profaned me" (Ezek. 13:19). Ezekiel's vision tells us that even the place God had claimed among his people as holy ground was being used to worship other gods. In a spiritual sense his home, the place on earth where he had chosen to dwell, had been broken into, spat on, defiled, trampled over, and scorned.

The holy God could no longer dwell in such a place and so, reluctantly but without a choice, he packed his bags and left his home among his people. In Ezekiel's vision he sees the glory of the Lord depart from the temple. The glory hovers at the edge of the temple; it's as if God is having one last look around before he finally leaves (Ezek. 10). It is because the holiness of God is offended that the glory of God leaves. God's address was no longer in Jerusalem, and this proved to have disastrous consequences. The people of Israel, just before Jerusalem was destroyed, thought their city was indestructible. How could anyone come close to conquering Jerusalem—it was where God lived! In 586 BC the king of Babylon crushed the city and destroyed the temple. This would have sent shockwaves throughout Israel—the place where God lived had been conquered! Ezekiel would have agreed that the place God chose to live was indestructible. The point was that he no longer lived in Jerusalem! The presence of God had left the temple.

The Presence Will Return ... Eventually

Having predicted the fall of Jerusalem, Ezekiel went on to prophesy about the day Israel would return from exile. In Ezekiel 40—48 he has a vision of a new temple being built and the glory of the Lord returning to dwell among his people. This vision carries echoes of the paradise of Eden; a river is seen flowing from the south side of the altar in the temple. In the Bible, water is symbolic of life and particularly of the Holy Spirit. It's when the presence of the living God returns to the temple that life returns to Israel. As the river flows out from the temple in the vision, the dry, parched, barren, dead land becomes rich and abundant, overflowing with goodness. Ezekiel tells us that "where the river flows everything will live" (Ezek. 47:9). Furthermore he prophesies that this sanctuary is to surpass the old one; the Lord intends to "put my sanctuary among them forever. My dwelling place will be with them; I will be their God, and they will be my people. Then the nations will know that I the LORD make Israel holy, when my sanctuary is among them forever" (Ezek. 37:26–28).

Eventually the people of Israel started to return from exile. One of the first things they did was begin to rebuild the temple at Jerusalem. This is recorded in the book of Ezra and Nehemiah. Ezra tells us that those who remembered the old temple wept when they saw the new one being built:

All the people gave a great shout of praise to the LORD,
because the foundation of the house of the LORD was

laid. But many of the older priests and Levites and
family heads, who had seen the former temple, wept
aloud when they saw the foundation of this temple
being laid, while many others shouted for joy. (Ezra
3:11–12)

Why did they weep? Nobody knows for sure. It could have been that the new temple was much smaller and plainer than the old temple; it could have been that they just didn't like the color scheme. It could have been, however, that the older priests who remembered the first temple realized that something was missing, or rather Someone: This time there is no account of God manifesting his presence.

Mike and I have visited some churches that have made our mouths water because of all the stuff they have: sound systems that would be an engineer's dream; lighting that wouldn't look out of place at the Queen's palace; soft, comfortable chairs; coffee shops and slick presentations. And yet, to be honest, sometimes we've been bored. Then we've sometimes been to other churches where, as we've walked through the door, we've thought, "This place could do with a coat of paint and a bit of air freshener." Yet as the meeting has started, it's impossible not to recognize it: the manifest presence of God. When God shows up, people don't care how hard the seats are! This is not to say we haven't encountered the manifest presence of God in some very nice buildings. But the point is that the presence of God, not the building, matters. The dedication of this new temple in Ezra 6 is different. The glory fell at the dedication of the tabernacle in the wilderness; it fell at the dedication of the first temple under

Solomon; yet it is notably absent in the dedication of the second temple. But what of Ezekiel's visions? Didn't he predict that the glory would return? Didn't he tell us that a river of life would flow? Perhaps the older priests were thinking he had got it wrong ...

Enter Jesus.

Emmanuel—The Presence Is with Us

> *In the beginning was the Word, and the Word was with God, and the Word was God. He was with God in the beginning. Through him all things were made; without him nothing was made that has been made. In him was life, and that light was the light of men.... The Word became flesh and made his dwelling among us. We have seen his glory ... (John 1:1–4, 14)*

The eternal God who made the entire universe, the One who sustains everything that surrounds you—your seat, this book, your hands, your eyes, your thoughts, your very breath—this God chose to no longer live behind a curtain in a building where only the chief priest could come once a year. This awesome, all-creating, all-sustaining God became a little Jewish guy. Instead of being surrounded by a curtain, he wore a diaper; instead of being ministered to by priests (the Jewish elite), he was brought gifts by a bunch of foreigners (the wise men); instead of smelling incense he smelled animal dung. The awesome God who could not be seen was stared at by shepherds from the nightshift. *The Message* translation of John 1 tells us that God "moved into the neighborhood" (v. 14).

To describe God as "a little Jewish guy" sounds a tad disrespectful, so before you write us a letter, let's check out Isaiah 53:2:

> *He grew up before him like a tender shoot, and like a root out of dry ground. He had no beauty or majesty to attract us to him, nothing in his appearance that we should desire him.*

So as God grew up, he looked like your average, first-century Jew. This means he did not have blond hair and blue eyes, nor was he six foot; in fact the God who was worshipped and ministered to by angels, the Holy of Holies, could be found brushing his own hair and wiping his own backside. The word *Emmanuel* means "God with us." It means God, not just standing alongside us, but God becoming like us in every way—except that he was without sin.

The technical term for God becoming human is *incarnation.* There's a whole branch of theology called Christology that is devoted to the subject of the nature of Christ. The bottom line is that the body of Jesus didn't carry God in the way a car carries a person. It wasn't that there was a "God part" and a "human part" to Jesus; he was totally God and totally human. When the woman who had a hemorrhage for twelve years touched his cloak, she didn't just touch human flesh, she touched God. The nails that pierced the hands and feet of Jesus nailed God himself to the cross. At the beginning of Matthew we read of the birth of Jesus, "All this took place to fulfill what the Lord had said through the prophet: 'The virgin will be with child and will give birth to a son, and they will call him Immanuel'— which means, 'God with us'" (Matt. 1:22–23; cf. Isa. 7:14).

Even more amazing is that God did not take on human flesh for thirty-three years and then chuck it as soon as he had the chance. After the resurrection he invited Thomas to touch the wounds in his hands and the hole in his side. He ascended to heaven as a human, and when the dead are raised on the last day, heaven will be populated by human beings. At the moment there is just one man in heaven, and his name is Jesus.

The Heavenly Presence

> *In my Father's house are many rooms; if it were not so, I would have told you. I am going there to prepare a place for you. And if I go and prepare a place for you, I will come back and take you to be with me that you also may be where I am. (John 14:2–3)*

How many times have we thought of this passage and imagined Jesus as an interior designer, going ahead to heaven to prepare each of our rooms—one can have New York Knicks wallpaper, another a king-sized bed? But if we read this passage carefully, the point is not what our room will look like—but that we will be where Jesus is. We so often wonder if heaven will have green fields and blue skies, and whether or not it will look like Colorado or Australia, but we miss the point: Heaven is to bask in the presence of God.

The great heroes of the Old Testament longed to soak in the presence of God. Exodus 33 tells us how Moses, who had been wandering around the desert with God for years, who had seen him do great miracles, who had been given the Ten Commandments, still cried out, "Now show me your glory" (v. 18). The same chapter tells us how Joshua, before he ever led God's people, "did not leave the tent" (v. 11) of God's presence. David cries out in Psalm 27:4:

> *One thing I ask of the LORD, this is what I seek: that*
> *I may dwell in the house of the LORD all the days of*
> *my life, to gaze upon the beauty of the LORD and to*
> *seek him in his temple.*

Because of Jesus we can experience the fulfillment of the longings of Moses, of Joshua, of David. This is part of a prayer Jesus prayed for us: "Father, I want those you have given me to be with me where I am, and to see my glory, the glory you have given me because you loved me before the creation of the world" (John 17:24). Jesus, Emmanuel, God with us, is God's answer to the heart-cry of humanity: "Now show me your glory."

The Presence Lives in Us

As Christians we believe that God is triune. This is the belief that our God is one God and yet at the same time exists, and has always existed, as three distinct Persons: God the Father, God the Son, and God the Holy Spirit. It is called the doctrine (teaching) of the Trinity. We believe in the Trinity not because the Bible explicitly states "God is one and God is three" but because of the way in which God is portrayed as working in the world and in relationship within himself. In Deuteronomy 6:4, God's people are told to recite the words, "The LORD our God, the LORD is one." Jesus himself also declares, "Hear, O Israel, the Lord our God, the Lord is one" (Mark 12:29). Yet at the same time, before humanity was even created, there were hints of a relationship within God himself. In the very first verse of Genesis where "God created the heavens and the earth," the word for God is not singular but plural. Toward the end of the creation story, God says, "Let us make man in our image, in our likeness …" (Gen. 1:26)—and he's not talking to the angels!

The storyline of the Persons of the Trinity does run throughout the Bible, but it is most explicit in the New Testament. The divinity of Jesus is pointed at in a number of ways throughout the Gospels. At the opening of John we are told that the Word (referring to Jesus) is God. Later Jesus received the confession of Thomas: "My Lord and my God!" (John 20:28). And in another place Jesus did not rebuke but received the worship of the disciples (Matt 14:33). Jesus even said of himself, "Before Abraham was born, I am" (John 8:58), and we then read that the Pharisees took up stones to throw at him. Why? Because they knew what he was saying. He was claiming to be God. He was referring to a conversation God had with Moses at the burning bush. Moses asked God, "'What shall I tell them [your name is]?' God said to Moses, 'I am who I am … [tell them] "I AM has sent me to you"'" (Ex. 3:13–14). Jesus had the outright cheek to say, "Before Abraham was born, I am." Whether or not you believed him, Jesus was undoubtedly claiming to be God.

There are also many scriptures that point to the divinity of the Holy Spirit. He is present and active at creation. He imparts spiritual gifts such as prophecy and healing, gifts that can only come from God. He is shown to be omnipresent (i.e., everywhere at once)—an attribute only of God. In Acts 5, when Ananias is caught lying, Peter says he is lying to "God" and elsewhere says he's lying to "the Holy

Spirit." The words God and Holy Spirit are used interchangeably, suggesting God and the Holy Spirit are one and the same.

The Persons of God are also shown to be in relationship with each other. For example, at the baptism of Jesus, as God the Son comes up out of the water, God the Spirit descends on him and God the Father speaks to him:

> *At that moment heaven was opened, and he saw the Spirit of God descending like a dove and lighting on him. And a voice from heaven said, "This is my Son, whom I love; with him I am well pleased." (Matt. 3:16–17)*

This is not God doing different things in different forms, but rather the different Persons of God actually interacting with each other. The Father, the Son, and the Holy Spirit are all fully and equally God. Paul prays in 2 Corinthians 13:14, "May the grace of the Lord Jesus Christ, and the love of God, and the fellowship of the Holy Spirit be with you all." Here and elsewhere in Scripture the blessing of Father, of Son, and of Holy Spirit is seen to be flowing from one divine source through three distinct Persons.

There is no simple way to understand the Trinity; here we must content ourselves with the understanding that the presence of each Person of the Trinity is the full presence of God. So it is that Jesus, as he prepares to leave the world, tells his disciples, "It is for your good that I am going away. Unless I go away, the Counselor will not come to you; but if I go, I will send him to you" (John 16:7). When Jesus refers to the Holy Spirit as "Counselor," another translation is "another like me" (see John 14:16), implying Jesus and the Holy Spirit are distinct but similar. It is good that Jesus goes and the Holy Spirit comes. This is not because the Holy Spirit has more of the presence of God—they are the same and equal. But while Jesus (the presence of God) stood next to his disciples, the Holy Spirit (the presence of God) *entered into* his disciples on the day of Pentecost.

Just as Jesus came into the world through the Holy Spirit resting on the virgin Mary, so too Jesus comes to be in us through the Holy Spirit resting on us. The Holy Spirit is the presence of God in us; he is also that which enables us to be in Christ and Christ to be in us: "God has chosen to make known among the Gentiles the glorious riches of this mystery, which is Christ in you, the hope of glory" (Col. 1:27).

A few years ago John V. Taylor wrote a book on the Holy Spirit called *The Go-Between God*. An amazing title for the Holy Spirit; he is God, and he goes between God the Father, God the Son, and us! When Bible translators are trying to translate the Scriptures into a completely new language, it's not always possible to find words that have the exact same meaning. In a remote area of China, some Bible translators got stuck when they realized the language had no words for "Holy Spirit." They sat and thought hard for a while, trying to come up with the nearest possible phrase. They decided that the best description in the language was "resident boss." So for a while in this area of China, the Trinity was described as the Father, the Son, and the Resident Boss! What a great name! The Holy Spirit is God living as Lord in us.

In the Old Testament the Holy Spirit comes upon prophets, priests, and kings. On the day of Pentecost, when Jesus' disciples were gathered together, the room suddenly shook, the wind started to howl, and they saw tongues of fire coming and resting on each other; the presence of God fell. Peter explained to the crowd of thousands that gathered at the commotion, "In the last days, God says, I will pour out my Spirit on all people" (Acts 2:17). The Holy Spirit is poured out on all of us! What's more, the Holy Spirit changes us. From the day of Pentecost onward, we see the disciples—a group of timid, fearful men who never quite seemed to get what Jesus was talking about—transformed into people who had boldness, power, authority, wisdom, and discernment. This was only because they were immersed in the Holy Spirit, because the presence of the living God came to live in them. It has always been the presence of God that makes the difference.

As I've mentioned, in June 2007, Mike and I traveled to Israel for the first time. It was amazing to visit all the places we'd read about for years. To walk on the old Roman road to Emmaus, to visit the place where David fought Goliath, and to stand next to Nehemiah's wall were very special moments. High on the list of memories is our visit to the Old City of Jerusalem and particularly to what is known by some as the Wailing Wall. This is part of the retaining wall that surrounded the now-destroyed temple. Every day for hundreds of years, Jews have been gathering there to pray for the Messiah to come. When we went, we joined hundreds who were praying against the wall, many nodding their heads, many reading scriptures, and we noticed thousands of prayers written on bits of paper and crammed into every crevice in the wall. As we prayed, we sensed that we were in a holy place—very near the site of Solomon's temple, where God's presence had rested. We thought to ourselves, *How utterly amazing:*

Almighty God lived here; this is a holy place!

Then it hit us. And we say this with all humility: God lives in Mike Pilavachi and God lives in Andy Croft; we are his holy temple. If you are a follower of Jesus, then God lives in you, too; you are a holy place. This is the amazing truth of what it is to be a Christian! We don't have to go to a special place to find God; he is within us! "Don't you know that you yourselves are God's temple and that God's Spirit lives in you?" (1 Cor. 3:16).

The Presence of Love and Holiness

In the Old Testament the emphasis appears to be upon the holiness, otherness, and majesty of God, who existed behind the curtain. In contrast to this, it can seem in the New Testament as if the emphasis is on the nearness, gentleness, and accessibility of God as revealed in Jesus. But God's holiness and awesomeness, and his tenderness and nearness, are two sides of the same coin. We can't grasp one without the other. For example, the disciple John appeared to have a very close and intimate relationship with Jesus; so close, in fact, he gave himself a nickname—the "beloved disciple." John actually went around saying, "I'm the disciple he loves!" The closeness of John to Jesus is illustrated by the fact that at the Last Supper he leaned with his head on Jesus' chest.

This same John had a vision of this same Jesus, which he describes in Revelation 1. It's as if he doesn't quite know how to describe what he sees; he ends this description by saying, "In his right hand he held seven stars, and out of his mouth came a sharp double-edged sword. His face was like the sun shining in all its brilliance" (v. 16). You get the impression that John didn't recognize his best friend. He then says, "When I saw him, I fell at his feet as though dead" (v. 17). John continues, "Then he placed his right hand on me ..." The same hand that John saw holding the stars in space was placed on John's head and quite possibly ruffled his hair. We might expect at this point that Jesus would whisper, "John, it's me, your friend ..." Instead he says this:

> *Do not be afraid. I am the First and the Last. I am*
> *the Living One; I was dead, and behold I am alive*
> *for ever and ever! And I hold the keys of death and*
> *Hades. (vv. 17–18)*

The same Jesus who can appear as "gentle Jesus, meek and mild," on whose chest we can lay our heads, is the one who holds the keys of life and death; in him is both the meekness and the majesty. We will never understand the meekness without the majesty or the majesty without the meekness. We will never fully comprehend his holiness without his love or his love without his holiness. When God makes himself present to us, he always comes in all of who he is. When he comes to be near to us, when he comes to be close to us, when he comes to live in us, he doesn't leave his holiness in heaven.

The Power of the Presence

The presence of the Holy Spirit in the lives of followers of Jesus causes three key things to happen:

The first is revelation of Jesus: "But the Counselor, the Holy Spirit, whom the Father will send in my name, will teach you all things and will remind you of everything I have said to you" (John 14:26). "When the Counselor comes, whom I will send to you from the Father, the Spirit of truth who goes out from the Father, he will testify about me" (John 15:26). "But when he, the Spirit of truth, comes, he will guide you into all truth. He will not speak on his own; he will speak only what he hears, and he will tell you what is yet to come. He will bring glory to me by taking from what is mine and making it known to you" (John 16:13–14).

The second is that the Holy Spirit gives us power to be witnesses. "But you will receive power when the Holy Spirit comes on you; and you will be my witnesses in Jerusalem, and in all Judea and Samaria, and to the ends of the earth" (Acts 1:8). From the day of Pentecost onward, it was obvious that the disciples had power to be witnesses; wherever they went, they did amazing miracles, preached effective sermons—and people became Christians. They could not have done this without God's presence. The power is in the presence.

The third is that the Holy Spirit comes, as his name would suggest, to make us holy, i.e., more like Jesus. Christianity is not a self-help course; it is a transformation. It was not the rituals or ceremony of the Old Testament temple that made it holy. What made it holy was God's presence. Similarly, that which makes us holy is not, at heart, anything that we might do but rather the presence of God in us.

> *Now the Lord is the Spirit, and where the Spirit*
> *of the Lord is, there is freedom. And we, who with*
> *unveiled faces all reflect the Lord's glory, are being*
> *transformed into his likeness with ever-increasing*

glory, which comes from the Lord, who is the Spirit.
(2 Cor. 3:17–18)

In Galatians 5:22–23 we read that "love, joy, peace, patience, kindness, goodness, faithfulness, gentleness and self-control" are described as "the fruit of the Spirit"—this is a great description of Jesus and those qualities that the Holy Spirit brings as he forms the character of Jesus in us.

The Key Is God's Presence

Just as it was God's presence leaving and returning in Ezekiel's visions of the temple that made the difference between the city being destroyed and the wilderness exploding with life, so too it is the presence of God that makes the difference for his temple today. The key to Christian living is not how clever, good-looking, funny, well dressed, or connected we are. The key is God's presence. Moses discovered this when at the burning bush he protested that he wasn't eloquent enough to fulfill the task that God had given him. God's response was not to give him a course of elocution lessons; God simply said, "I will go with you." After the death of Moses, when God commissioned Joshua to lead the people into the Promised Land, he knew Joshua was afraid. He didn't calm his fears by sending him a giant army; instead he said, "I will be with you." David, the most successful general and greatest warrior in Israel's history, sings of the secret of his confidence: "Even though I walk through the valley of the shadow of death, I will fear no evil …" Why would David fear no evil? "… for you are with me" (Ps. 23:4).

So God's presence is everywhere; part of the definition of being God is to be omnipresent. However, we have also seen that, throughout the Old Testament, God manifested his presence at specific times and specific places. One word for this manifest presence is *glory*. Two thousand years ago the glory of God and the holiness of God were given their ultimate expression in the Person of Jesus, Emmanuel. We've seen in the Old Testament that God, by his Spirit, indwelt prophets, priests, and kings. We see from the day of Pentecost that the Holy Spirit, God's holy presence, comes to dwell in all his people. Those who have revelation of Jesus as Lord, those who have power to be witnesses to him, and those who are becoming more like him have the presence of God living in them.

All of this is a work in progress; one day it will be complete.

> *And I heard a loud voice from the throne saying, "Now the dwelling of God is with men, and he will live with them. They will be his people, and God himself will be with them and be their God. He will wipe every tear from their eyes. There will be no more death or mourning or crying or pain, for the old order of things has passed away." (Rev. 21:3–4)*

And so in the end, God has his way. At the beginning of Genesis we saw God created human beings to live in his presence, and yet after they sinned, they hid in the garden. The first question God asks humanity in the Bible is, "Where are you?" A great theme in the story of the Bible is God longing and finding a way to be present among his people. Today the presence that used to walk around Eden, the presence that fell on Solomon's temple, the presence that every hero of the Old Testament sought, lives in us. The promise for the future is that one day his omnipresence, his manifest presence, and his indwelling presence will be one and the same; and in that presence all our sickness, our sorrow, and our tears will be wiped away.

Presence Storyline Paperchase:

God longs to be present with his people:
- Genesis 1—3 (God in Eden, present with his people)
- Exodus 3:5 (burning bush)

Israel must make an effort:
- Exodus 25—30 (tabernacle instructions)
- Leviticus 23:26–30 (Day of Atonement)
- Exodus 40:24–35 (the glory enters the tabernacle)

The presence is everything:
- 1 Samuel 4—6 (presence captured and recovered)
- 2 Chronicles 5—7 (God moves into the temple)
- Exodus 33:14–23 (nothing but his presence will distinguish us)

The presence is lost:
- Ezekiel 10 (vision of the glory departing)

The presence will return ... eventually:
- Ezra, especially 3:11–12; 6 (rebuilding the temple, but no glory falls)

— Ezekiel 40—48 (vision of the new temple and the river of life)

Emmanuel:

- John 1:1–4, 14 (the Word becomes flesh)
- Isaiah 53:2 (there is nothing to attract us to him)
- Matthew 1:23; compare Isaiah 7:14 (God with us, as prophesied!)

The heavenly presence:

- John 14:2–3; 17:24
- Psalm 27:4 (heaven is to bask in the presence of God)

The presence lives in us:

- Deuteronomy 6:4; compare Mark 12:29 (the oneness of God)
- Genesis 1:26; Matthew 3:16–17 (hints of relationship in God, suggesting his threeness)
- John 16:7 (the Holy Spirit—God's presence—is promised)
- Acts 2 (the Holy Spirit is poured out on all people)
- 1 Corinthians 3:16 (we are God's temple)

The presence of love and holiness:

- Revelation 1:16–18 (awesomeness of the one who was John's close personal friend)

The power of the presence:

- John 16:13–14 (revelation)
- Acts 1:8 (to be witnesses)
- 2 Corinthians 3:17–18 (to transform us)

The key is God's presence:

- Psalm 23:4 (God with us is reason not to fear)
- Revelation 21:3–4 (dwelling in the presence)

Discussion Questions:

- Which section, as we journey through the presence storyline, speaks to you the most? Why?
- How does the tension of God's holiness and his longing to be near us relate to what happened on the cross?
- In Scripture, when God's presence falls, people notice. What evidence is there in your life of the power and presence of God?

4

The Kingdom Storyline

Imagine Her Majesty is paying a royal visit to your street. What do you do? Here in England the flags come out in every window and everything is freshly painted. As the royal carriage comes down the road, you cheer, bow, or curtsy; you may even sing the national anthem. You stand in line, she offers you her hand, and you call her "ma'am" and bow your head. You treat her with the dignity, respect, and reverence that she deserves. While all this is happening, there might be a nagging thought at the back of your mind. She may be Queen, but we all know Gordon, our prime minister, has the power. She is the figurehead, we bow and curtsy, but we don't do a thing she says—for that we look to the prime minister. This is a worryingly accurate picture of how we sometimes treat Jesus. We cheer, we wave, we bow, we say, "You're our King," but then there's a thought at the back of our minds: "But I'm the prime minister of my life." The kingdom of God is not based on the British constitution; it's altogether different. As we will see in this chapter, Jesus expects to be both the King and Prime Minister of our lives.

After Jesus the kingdom is arguably the central theme in the whole of Scripture. Jesus talks about the kingdom more than any other subject. He begins his ministry with the announcement, "The time has come … the kingdom of God is near" (Mark 1:15). Most of Jesus' parables were stories of the kingdom. He would often begin, "The kingdom of God is like …" His miracles and healings were demonstrations that the kingdom had come. The prayer that Jesus taught us to pray, the prayer that Christians have been praying for two thousand years, is, "Your kingdom come, your will be done."

What are we actually praying for when we ask for the kingdom? Why did Jesus spend so much of his time talking about it? What is the kingdom of God? To understand what Jesus meant and what his listeners heard when he came announcing the kingdom, we need to pick up the storyline in the book of Genesis …

The garden of Eden, as with the other storylines, is our picture of what God originally intended. In the kingdom of Eden, man and woman had close fellowship with God. They had all that they needed in abundance, they lived under his rule and protection, and they were given authority over the whole earth. Yet they chose, by eating the fruit that gives knowledge of good and evil, to become independent, to become rulers of their own lives. It was this choice that meant they were no longer able to stay in Eden; those who don't allow God to be their King can hardly expect to be part of his kingdom.

The Kingdom Forged

God, as we have said so often, loves us deeply and longs for relationship with us. This love is the reason he set about reestablishing his kingdom. But for God to have relationship with us, he has to be our King; he is God, and he cannot be anything else. To reestablish his kingdom, God first set out to win a people. We pick up the storyline in the book of Exodus, where we find the children of Israel ruled by Pharaoh. Pharaoh was a nasty king and treated the Israelites like dirt. God appeared at the burning bush to Moses, saying, "I have heard the cries of my people." He told Moses he was going to war! He was going to win back his people from Pharaoh. God had to fight two battles....

The first was the spiritual battle—the God of heaven took on the gods of the Egyptians (Exodus 7—11). The Egyptians had some pretty strange gods. The weirdest was the frog, which represented the god of fertility. Anyone who has a pond in their back garden will understand why. Mike has spent many a pleasant spring afternoon sitting by his pond watching two frogs do the business. Within a short space of time, his pond is overrun by tadpoles. Without a doubt frogs are fertile little creatures. How does God deal with the god of fertility? He sends the frogs into overdrive. Suddenly there are millions of them—a plague all over Egypt. Another Egyptian "god" was the river Nile. God decides to kill the Nile. He turns it to blood, and it symbolically bleeds to death. The sun was the great god of Egypt and was blotted out by the darkness sent by the Lord. Pharaoh was regarded as a god in Egypt; the Lord killed his firstborn. Each plague was a victory in God's spiritual battle.

The physical battle soon followed. At last Pharaoh agreed to let the Israelites go. They fled, but no sooner had they left than Pharaoh changed his mind. He got the army and raced after the Israelites. The Israelites found themselves trapped—on the one side they had the army of Egypt, on the other the Red Sea. What did God do? Did he tell Moses to get the Israelites into battle forma-tion while he dropped machine guns from heaven? No. God, all by himself, was going to win the people of Israel. He told Moses to stretch out his hand over the Red Sea; it parted, and the Israelites crossed to safety. When the Egyptians tried to follow, the waters crashed down, killing them. Once they'd reached the other side the Israelites joyfully sang a song of salvation that ends with the words, "The LORD will reign for ever and ever" (Ex. 15:18). This was the first proclamation by Israel that the Lord was King. God had done it! He'd won a people!

Having won Israel for himself and become their King, God gave them his laws to obey (Ex. 19—20).

The next thing he wanted to do was win a land for them. The King led his people through the desert for forty years, and eventually they arrived at the edge of the Promised Land. The first city that stood in their way was Jericho. The Lord told the people of Israel to march around the city for seven days. They were to do so with the priests in front blowing their horns and carrying the ark of the covenant, which was both the symbol and the reality of God's presence in their midst. The key phrase is found in Joshua 6:2: "Then the LORD said to Joshua, 'See, I have delivered Jericho into your hands, along with its king and its fighting men.'" The walls of Jericho collapsed on the seventh day without a shot being fired. The Lord did as he promised and gave his people victory. It was the Lord who won the victory, and this pattern was repeated again and again throughout the conquest of the land. Battles were won only when the King was with his people. He conquered a land for them.

The first picture of the kingdom in the Old Testament is that of the kingdom forged. God, longing for relationship with humanity, won a people for himself and a land for his people. He gave them his laws and established the kingdom of Israel, to which all the kingdoms of the earth would be able to look and see his glory.

The Kingdom Flourishing

The second great Old Testament picture of what the kingdom meant for Israel was the reign of David and his son Solomon (1 Sam. 16—1 Kings 11). In 1 Samuel 16, God told his prophet Samuel to go to a little town called Bethlehem. He would find a boy whom he was to anoint with oil to be king of Israel. This boy was David, the "anointed one" (*Messiah* in Hebrew). Psalm 2 (known as a messianic psalm) talks of the Lord and his anointed one. The Lord says, "I have installed my King on Zion, my holy hill…. You are my Son; today I have become your Father. Ask of me, and I will make the nations your inheritance, the ends of the earth your possession" (vv. 6–8).

The Lord chose to rule his people through an anointed son. David won tons of battles; while he and his son Solomon were kings, Israel did pretty well! They were the superpower of the region; their economy prospered, and they lived in *shalom*, or "wholeness." The picture of the kingdom we see here is one of a kingdom battling and succeeding. A kingdom that hugely extends its boundaries and that has a wonderfully fruitful life under God's blessing. The era of David and Solomon is one of the kingdom at the top of the Premier League—rich, powerful, prospering, and at peace; the kingdom flourishing. Then … disaster!

The Kingdom Falls

Most of the kings after David and Solomon turned from the Lord. As a result the King of heaven withdrew his protection. He allowed the kings of Assyria and Babylon to invade and defeat his people (see 2 Kings 17 and 25). When they had been brought out of Egypt, the Israelites gained the Promised Land, they received the Law, and they built the temple. The land, Law, and temple were signs of the kingdom, signs of the fact that Yahweh had become their King and they his people. They were the center of Israel's special relationship with God. When Israel was defeated, they lost the land, they were forced to obey the laws of another king, and the temple was destroyed. The great disaster, however, was what all this pointed to—Israel, "God's people," had lost their King. The Israelites now had nothing to distinguish them from all the peoples of the earth, nothing that set them apart, nothing that marked them out as being subjects of King Yahweh. In exile the picture of the flourishing kingdom faded into memory, and the Israelites were left to wonder if the King of heaven would ever return. With the beginning of exile, the kingdom fell.

The Kingdom Foretold

As the dust of the fallen kingdom settled, there arose, among the ashes of God's people, a spring of hope. It began, even before the exile, as a trickle, but it was in the depths of Israel's despair that God raised up men such as Isaiah and Ezekiel. These prophets thundered to God's demoralized people the message that they were to take heart. They had not been abandoned by their King. Yahweh would again raise up an anointed son, a Messiah like David. His kingdom, however, would be even greater than David's. The kingdom wasn't simply to be restored; it was to be better than it had ever been before.

One of these prophecies is found in Isaiah 11. Isaiah speaks of the King who will return:

> *The Spirit of the LORD will rest on him—the Spirit of wisdom and of understanding, the Spirit of counsel and of power, the Spirit of knowledge and of the fear of the LORD—and he will delight in the fear of the LORD. He will not judge by what he sees with his eyes, or decide by what he hears with his ears; but with righteousness he will judge the needy, with justice he will give decisions for the poor of the earth. (Isa. 11:2–4)*

Isaiah continues:

> *The wolf will live with the lamb, the leopard will lie down with the goat, the calf and the lion and yearling together; and a little child will lead them. The cow will feed with the bear, their young will lie down together, and the lion will eat straw like the ox. The infant will play near the hole of the cobra, and the young child put his hand into the viper's nest. They will neither harm nor destroy on all my holy mountain, for the earth will be full of the knowledge of the LORD as the waters cover the sea. (Isa. 11:6–9)*

God's people in exile began to look forward to this amazing King and his promised kingdom: a kingdom of justice, fairness, and peace;

a kingdom in which it will no longer be the survival of the fittest. This is the first hint that the kingdom to come will be an upside-down kingdom—"a little child will lead them." These prophecies form the picture of the kingdom foretold.

The Kingdom Forgotten?

On one level the predictions of Isaiah and Ezekiel that the Israelites would be saved proved to be true. The Israelites returned to the land and rebuilt the walls of Jerusalem and the temple. Yet, looking at the temple, they would have seen that it was not greater, but rather smaller than the original. They would have known that they still had to obey the laws of a foreign king (they were now ruled by Persia), and they would have realized it didn't look likely they'd get their own king any time soon. The returned exiles no doubt thought to themselves, "What's become of the grand prophecies of Ezekiel and the others?" They may have perhaps muttered under their breath, "That guy Isaiah told us it was going to be amazing; why is it like this?" The voices of the prophets seemed to have been silenced, and for hundreds of years the people may well have wondered, "What have we done? God won't even speak to us anymore!" (This was the period between the end of the Old and beginning of the New Testament.)

The kingdom had been forged, it had flourished, and it had fallen. A new kingdom had been foretold, and Israel had been saved from exile—but the promises of the new and better kingdom had yet to bear fruit. Then four hundred years of silence. What had happened to the promised better kingdom? Had it been exaggerated or forgotten? No one really knew.

The Kingdom Fulfilled

(We know this is stretching the letter *f* to its limits, but we've gotten this far so we won't quit now....)

Then one day a slightly nutty-looking guy with weird fashion sense and a weirder diet began to preach in the wilderness. He said, "I ain't the King, but he's on his way!" Soon after, while he was baptizing people in the Jordan, John spotted Jesus, pointed to him, and proclaimed, "Look, the Lamb of God, who takes away the sin of the world!" (John 1:29). In other words John said, "There he is, that's him!" Jesus began his ministry by announcing, "The kingdom of God is near" (Mark 1:15). The four hundred years of silence was at an end.

What did Jesus mean? Reading the Gospels, you could easily think that Jesus was obsessed with the kingdom; it was all he talked about. Perhaps one reason many of us find it difficult to understand what the phrase "kingdom of God" means is that Jesus taught as much about the kingdom through his actions as he did through his words. Right at the start of his ministry, Jesus informed us the kingdom of God is about deeds as well as words. In Luke 4, Jesus entered the synagogue in Nazareth, his home town. He went to the front, picked up a scroll, opened it to Isaiah 61, and read:

> "*The Spirit of the Lord is on me, because he has anointed me to preach good news to the poor. He has sent me to proclaim freedom for the prisoners and recovery of sight for the blind, to release the oppressed, to proclaim the year of the Lord's favor.*" *Then he rolled up the scroll, gave it back to the*

attendant and sat down. The eyes of everyone in the
synagogue were fastened on him, and he began by
saying to them, "Today this scripture is fulfilled in
your hearing." (Luke 4:18–21)

Jesus wasn't just reading Isaiah in the sense of "Wouldn't it be nice if this happened?" He was firmly announcing, first, that he was the anointed one—the Christ, the Messiah. Secondly, he was proclaiming what the kingdom would look like. For the next three years the blind began to see, the oppressed were released, and good news was preached to the poor. In the end every government is judged by what they do, not just what they say—what Jesus did showed what the kingdom of God would be like....

The Deeds of the King

The deeds of Jesus in Mark's gospel speak clearly of the kingdom. Why was it that Jesus called twelve disciples, rather than eleven or thirteen? Was it just his favorite number? It was clearly a reference to the twelve tribes of Israel. As the twelve tribes made up the kingdom people of God, so Jesus was saying that he was forming a new kingdom people.

If one of us went up to a stranger in the grocery store and said, "Come, follow me!" and then marched out into the parking lot, the odds are they wouldn't follow us back to the car. When Jesus went up to strangers and said, "Come, follow me!" they obeyed! Jesus had authority, and this authority was recognized: "The people were amazed at his teaching, because he taught them as one who had authority, not as the teachers of the law" (Mark 1:22). It was because of this authority that when Jesus said "jump," whether it was to a fisherman or a wave, they replied, "How high?" Jesus had the authority of a king, and he didn't need a crown to show it—people recognized it instinctively.

This authority is also shown at the end of Mark 4 when Jesus calms the storm. "He got up, rebuked the wind and said to the waves, 'Quiet! Be still!' Then the wind died down and it was completely calm" (v. 39). The Jewish people saw the sea as representing chaos and opposition to the rule of God. God's rule over the waters of chaos and his kingship are sung of in Psalm 29:10: "The LORD sits enthroned over the flood; the LORD is enthroned as King forever." It was Jesus, as King, who ruled over the wind and the waves.

Immediately after this incident, Jesus arrives at the region of the Gerasenes. Here he casts out a legion of demons from a man whom no one else had previously been able to subdue. By doing, this Jesus was in effect saying, "I'm the King and this is a demonstration of my kingdom." In fact, in Matthew 12:28, Jesus taught, "If I drive out demons by the Spirit of God, then the kingdom of God has come upon you."

Later in Mark 5, as Jesus was walking through a bustling crowd, a woman who had been bleeding for years crept up and touched the edge of his coat and was instantly healed. A few verses later Jesus raised Jairus's dead daughter to life. He was the King who had authority over sickness and health, over life and death.

In chapter 6 we see King Herod in his palace throwing a banquet and beheading John the Baptist. The unjust king is having an extravagant time with his elite guests. In contrast the very next story is of Jesus feeding the five thousand in the wilderness. Mark wants us to see the difference between Herod in his palace with his mates, the ruling class, and Jesus in the wilderness with the multitudes. Jesus' kingdom is for everyone!

The feeding of the five thousand parallels a picture in the Old Testament; the people followed Jesus into the wilderness, just as the Israelites had followed Yahweh into the desert two thousand years earlier. As Yahweh fed them with manna in the wilderness, so Jesus, in the wilderness, miraculously multiplied a little boy's picnic. After all had eaten there were twelve baskets of food left over. This can be taken as a picture of the abundance of God's kingdom; the people ate till they were stuffed, and there were still leftovers (although, admittedly, Mike was not present!). The kingdom of Herod, cruel and unjust, is set in contrast to the kingdom of Jesus, where, like the Old Testament ideal, the ruler provides for and teaches his people.

Have you ever wondered why there's the story in Mark 8 where Jesus feeds only four thousand with a slightly bigger picnic? It seems like a bit of an anti-climax after five thousand! But the story is not there to tell us that Jesus had lost his touch as a miracle caterer. The feeding of the five thousand was in a completely Jewish area. The feeding of the four thousand took place in the region of the Decapolis (the Ten Cities), a predominantly Gentile area. This hints heavily that the kingdom was truly to spread beyond the Jewish nation. In fact, right at the beginning of the whole story, God said to Abraham that through his offspring "all peoples on earth will be blessed" (Gen. 12:3). Part of Israel's calling was that they were to be the nation to which all the nations would look and see the glory of Yahweh. That's why they were told in their law to welcome strangers and offer hospitality.

Additionally there are hints throughout the Old Testament that it was through Israel that Yahweh intended to reach all the nations. Zechariah 8:23 suggests this: "In those days ten men from all languages and nations will take firm hold of one Jew by the hem of his robe and say, 'Let us go with you, because we have heard that God is with you.'"

We get more hints of the all-inclusive nature of Jesus' kingdom when we glimpse one of the few times Jesus loses his temper. It's when he walks into the outer court of the temple in Jerusalem and finds it has been turned into a market. Enraged, he turns over the tables of the money changers and drives out all who are selling things. Did Jesus have a problem with selling things in the temple? Should we ban book sales in our churches? No, that wasn't what made Jesus angry. The outer court was the one place that was reserved for the Gentiles to come and pray, and with market stalls there it would have been pretty difficult to focus on God. That's why Jesus quoted the prophets Isaiah and Jeremiah, "Is it not written: 'My house will be called a house of prayer for all nations'? But you have made it 'a den of robbers'" (Mark 11:17). The kingdom that Jesus was advancing was to go beyond the Jewish nation.

After Jesus' resurrection the disciples asked him, "Lord, are you at this time going to restore the kingdom to Israel?" (Acts 1:6). He replied:

> *It is not for you to know the times or dates the Father has set by his own authority. But you will receive power when the Holy Spirit comes on you; and you will be my witnesses in Jerusalem, and in all Judea*

and Samaria, and to the ends of the earth. (Acts 1:7–8)

Even though the disciples still didn't completely get it, Jesus was telling them that this was for everyone to the ends of the earth. Even France! The disciples were told to tell the whole earth that the King had arrived.

The Titles of the King

Jesus had loads of titles, and it can be a bit confusing sometimes. It would have been simpler if he'd just stuck with one! Actually each of these titles has a meaning behind it. Jesus' favorite name for himself was "Son of Man." At first this can seem a little disappointing—Son of God would have been much cooler and grander! In fact this title is amazing, and it has its roots in the book of Daniel:

> *In my vision at night I looked, and there before me was one like a son of man, coming with the clouds of heaven. He approached the Ancient of Days and was led into his presence. He was given authority, glory and sovereign power; all peoples, nations and men of every language worshiped him. His dominion is an everlasting dominion that will not pass away, and his kingdom is one that will never be destroyed. (Dan. 7:13–14)*

The people of Israel were looking for the Son of Man, who, in their minds, was to be the same person as the Messiah, who would have an everlasting kingdom. Jesus deliberately uses that title to say, "This is me, I'm the King!"

Paul's favorite title for Jesus was *Christ*. It's easy for us to think of the word Christ simply as Jesus' surname, but it was no such thing! As we've already mentioned, the word literally means "anointed one," and in the Hebrew is translated *Messiah*. Israel had been waiting since the exile for God's Messiah to come and save them. Paul was pushing the point home—this is him!

Another title for Jesus is "Son of David," yet Jesus himself points to his being greater than David (Mark 12:35–37). David's kingdom lasted for a short time; the kingdom of the Son of David is to last forever.

The Ethics of the King

Jesus announced the principles of behavior that were to be expected in his kingdom. These have proven to be different from those expected in any other society on earth. Jesus outlined this in what is known as the Sermon on the Mount. Here are a few extracts of Jesus' "rules for living":

> *But I tell you who hear me: Love your enemies, do good to those who hate you, bless those who curse you, pray for those who mistreat you. If someone strikes you on one cheek, turn to him the other also. If someone takes your cloak, do not stop him from taking your tunic. Give to everyone who asks you, and if anyone takes what belongs to you, do not demand it back. (Luke 6:27–30)*

This was revolutionary teaching! No one had heard anything like this before. He continues: "Do not judge, and you will not be judged. Do not condemn, and you will not be condemned. Forgive, and you will be forgiven. Give, and it will be given to you" (vv. 37–38).

Jesus not only announced a new way of living, but demonstrated it himself. In John 8:1–11 some men brought a woman caught in adultery to Jesus and asked, "In the Law Moses commanded us to stone such women. Now what do you say?" (v. 5). Jesus responded: "If any one of you is without sin, let him be the first to throw a stone at her" (v. 7). They dropped their stones and left, one by one. Then "Jesus straightened up and asked her, 'Woman, where are they? Has no one condemned you?' 'No one, sir,' she said. 'Then neither do I condemn you,' Jesus declared. 'Go now and leave your life of sin'" (vv. 10–11).

Here Jesus is showing that the kingdom of God is not about judging one another but showing mercy.

In John 13, Jesus did something you would never expect a king to do: "Jesus knew that the Father had put all things under his power, and that he had come from God and was returning to God; so he … began to wash his disciples' feet" (vv. 3–5). Back in that day the guy that did the foot washing was the lowest of the servants. In order to wash feet, you had to bow. Jesus bowed in front of his disciples, and then he told them, "I have set you an example that you should do as I have done for you" (v. 15). We are told that the cream rises to the top. Jesus demonstrated that in his kingdom it sinks to the bottom. In every other society on earth, the leaders are treated the best, with chauffeurs, security guards, aides, and secretaries all over the place. Jesus said and demonstrated that the ruler is the one who serves. He was the servant King, and his kingdom is the upside-down kingdom. Jesus said loud and clear: "In my kingdom it's not about the love of power but the power of love." In all of this, Jesus was coloring in the outline sketched in Isaiah 11.

This isn't just a discussion of what a nice guy Jesus was. His life is a challenge and example to our lives! The subjects (us) are to follow the King. We are to strive afresh to love those we don't like, to wash feet, to lay down the power play and political games of the world, and instead proceed with kindness, humility, and generosity. We are living in a kingdom where we are free from the burden of always having to get our own way.

In the Old Testament we saw the picture of the kingdom forged, Israel rescued by God and brought into the land he had won for them. Then we saw the kingdom flourish under David and Solomon. We saw the kingdom fall as Israel was conquered and taken into exile. The final picture in the Old Testament is that of the kingdom, greater than David's, foretold. The people of Israel looked for this promise to be fulfilled when they returned from exile; they were disappointed. The words and actions of Jesus see the beginning of this fulfillment. Just as Yahweh fought and won a battle against Pharaoh, setting his people free, so Jesus on the cross fought and won a battle against sin, setting us free. Just as the reign of David and Solomon saw a period of peace and wholeness in Israel, so the reign of Jesus saw an invitation to know a peace that is beyond understanding.

In his titles, his deeds, and his ethics, Jesus deafeningly broke the four hundred years of silence. The King arrived, and he came announcing, "The kingdom of God is near." When Jesus began his ministry, he began to reestablish the kingdom of God, not by conquering countries and empires, but by conquering the hearts of people.

The Now and Not-yet Kingdom

So far it's been fairly straightforward, but, as no doubt some of you will have noticed, we seem to have hit a bit of a problem. If Jesus has conquered sin, why do we still have to battle with it every day? If Jesus reigns, why are our own lives often like a roller coaster? The picture of the kingdom of God in Eden is one of perfection—it's full of good fruit, the animals obey us, and God's presence is everywhere. We know the kingdom of God is meant to be like the powerful reigns of David and Solomon. Yet in another sense all of us can see that, in our own lives and in the world around us, the kingdom of God is far from the perfect reality of Eden. Was Jesus being overly optimistic? Did he jump the gun when he announced the kingdom of God? Has the kingdom failed?

Christians have been wrestling with this problem for ages. Some think that all the perfections of the kingdom are ours to receive now; if we only had faith in God and obeyed him, he would drop mansions, Ferraris, and football season tickets from heaven, and a parking space would always miraculously appear whenever we asked. This is what is known as "prosperity gospel" teaching. It teaches that the kingdom is already here in its completion; the only ingredient lacking is our faith and obedience!

Others think the opposite: Though we have been "saved," the kingdom of God on earth is wishful thinking; it won't be until we're in heaven that we receive any concrete sign of the King's reign. God doesn't intervene at all in a supernatural way in the world (i.e., we cannot expect miracles); we just need to cling on and hope for the best till we limp into heaven. The extreme of this teaching is that Jesus will one day return to a tiny church that will be persecuted in a world full of evil, and he will rescue the few who remain just in time. This could be described as a "poverty gospel."

Our experience is that neither the prosperity nor the poverty gospel satisfies—fortunately this also seems to be the teaching of Jesus and the whole New Testament.

The Kingdom of God Is Now

Having been asked by the Pharisees when the kingdom of God would come, Jesus replied that "the kingdom of God is within you" (Luke 17:21). This phrase is better translated "the kingdom of God is among you." Through stories, often following the formula "the kingdom of God is like …," Jesus would clarify what he meant. Stories of seed sown that yielded a harvest, of mustard seeds growing into huge trees, and of small amounts of yeast causing whole lumps of bread to rise, painted a picture of a dynamic kingdom emerging from a small beginning. It was this small beginning, this carpenter from Galilee, that the Pharisees had missed. Eating bread (Luke 14:15) and drinking wine (Mark 14:25) were signs of the kingdom of God. "John the Baptist came neither eating bread nor drinking wine" (Luke 7:33), but Jesus arrived eating and drinking. Those who'd missed the fact that the kingdom of God was in their midst called him "a glutton and a drunkard, a friend of tax collectors and 'sinners'" (Matt. 11:19; Luke 7:34).

Jesus clearly teaches through word and deed that the kingdom of God has arrived. The invitation he made, and the invitation that stands true today, is that all who repent, break off other allegiances, and accept God as their King will be welcomed into the kingdom with rejoicing. The words of Jesus echo through the Scriptures to us today—the kingdom of God is among us.

The Kingdom of God Is Not Yet

In other illustrations Jesus told of a future feast. He told parables of extravagant banquets and wedding feasts that will take place and to which many are invited. This feast is a picture of the final judgment, the day when believers are separated from unbelievers; an event we know is to take place in the future (Matt. 22:1–14). Jesus also told the parable of the ten minas in Luke 19:11–27. In this parable a master gives each servant a gift that they are to do with as they see fit. The master travels to a distant country where he is made king, and then he returns home. Luke himself tells us that the reason Jesus told this parable was because "the people thought that the kingdom of God was going to appear at once" (19:11). In other words Jesus was making the point to the people around him that the kingdom of God in its fullness was not going to be brought about straightaway.

Often when we read the Bible, perhaps because it was written in the past, we can think it only tells stories of past events. This is not the case; the second halves of these parables of Jesus have yet to happen. We've received the invitation to the banquet, but the actual banquet has yet to take place; Jesus has ascended into heaven but he has yet to return, with heaven and in his glory, as King. The book of Revelation, at the end of the Bible, is not only a book that narrates the present age; it also contains a vision of the future kingdom of God. In this vision the perfected kingdom is promised. When that time arrives, as in Eden, "the dwelling of God is with men, and he will live with them. They will be his people, and God himself will be with them and be their God" (Rev. 21:3). Furthermore, "He will wipe every tear from their eyes. There will be no more death or mourning or crying or pain, for the old order of things has passed away" (v. 4).

Here, then, we have a picture of the kingdom that is yet to arrive, when the death, pain, suffering, hunger, thirst, sickness, and loneliness we see in the world around us will be finished. The foretold kingdom of the Old Testament will arrive in its fullness, and the angels in heaven will declare, "The kingdom of the world has become the kingdom of our Lord and of his Christ, and he will reign for ever and ever" (Rev. 11:15).

It's easy to see why Christians spend a lot of time arguing about this subject! Scripture tells us that the promised kingdom has arrived; it also tells us that the complete fulfillment of the promises of the kingdom is still in the future. The mistake that could be made is that we tend to one extreme or the other—to say either that the kingdom has already arrived in all its fullness or that the kingdom isn't concretely here at all and God does not intervene in a supernatural way in the world. If we swing to either extreme, we miss the tension held in the Bible. Paul speaks of this tension many times; here is one example:

> *Rather, as servants of God we commend ourselves in*
> *every way ... through glory and dishonor, bad report*
> *and good report; genuine, yet regarded as impostors;*
> *known, yet regarded as unknown; dying, and yet*

we live on; beaten, and yet not killed; sorrowful, yet
always rejoicing; poor, yet making many rich; having
nothing, and yet possessing everything. (2 Cor. 6:4,
8–10)

For Paul the kingdom of God has most definitely arrived, but its complete fulfillment is still in the future. It is this now-and-not-yet aspect that means he can be sorrowful and yet always rejoicing and he can have nothing while possessing everything. The storyline of the kingdom that we pick up in the Bible is the picture of the kingdom now and not yet.

Many of us are too young to remember the end of the Second World War, yet it provides a helpful illustration as to the situation of the now-and-not-yet kingdom. The decisive battle in the war was on D-day. The Allies invaded France and pushed the Germans back. They formed a base in German territory into which they could safely pour thousands of troops. Once this foothold had been established, the war was effectively over; it was merely a matter of time before Berlin, the German headquarters, was conquered. However, the war did not officially end until VE Day (Victory in Europe Day) some months later. The shocking statistic is that more people died between D-day and VE Day than had died in the other four years of the war put together!

When Jesus died on the cross, the decisive battle was won. The kingdom arrived with the coming of Jesus, and we live in a time when sin is defeated and we are free from its clutches. We live in a time when, if we pray for healing, some people get healed; a time when some people become Christians; a time when God does bless us with his peace; and a time when every now and then we do get a parking space. D-day has happened, Jesus is victorious. On the other hand VE Day has yet to come. Some people don't get healed, many people are not remotely interested in Christianity, and we ourselves experience long times of spiritual hardship. Between D-day and VE Day there are many casualties.

Where does this leave us? Why bother praying at all? Why bother trying to live a life of the kingdom if the kingdom isn't yet fully here? The simple answer to such questions is that if Jesus is our King, we are to live to his standards. We are a people of the future kingdom of God. We are to live lives of the future in the present. The challenge is that if it's not good enough for the future kingdom of God, it's not good enough for the present. So when we see someone sick, we pray that God would heal them; when we see someone outside the kingdom, we invite them in; when we see someone in pain, we do all that we can to wipe the tears from their eyes. The kingdom storyline began with the kingdom in Eden; it will end with the perfect kingdom in Revelation. We are called to live in the kingdom now and not yet.

Kingdom Storyline Paperchase:

Old Testament

Eden:
 – Genesis 2—3

The kingdom forged:
 – Exodus 7—14 (wins a people)

— Exodus 20 (gives them his law)

— Joshua 6 (conquers a land)

The kingdom flourishing:

— 1 Samuel 16 (anointing of David) to 1 Kings 10 (height of Solomon's power) (See also 1 Chronicles 11 to 2 Chronicles 9.)

The kingdom falls:

— 2 Kings 17 (fall of Israel)

— 2 Kings 25 (fall of Judah)

The kingdom foretold:

— Isaiah 11

The kingdom forgotten?

— Seeming failure of promises and the silence before Jesus

New Testament

The kingdom foretold:

(This is happening throughout the New Testament, but highlighted in this chapter are ...)

The deeds of the King:

— especially Mark 4—8

The titles of the King:

— Son of Man; compare Daniel 7:13

- Christ—anywhere in Paul's letters!
- Son of David; compare Mark 12:35–37

The ethics of the King:

- Luke 6; Matthew 5—7 (Sermon on the Mount)
- John 8 (woman in adultery)
- John 13 (Jesus washing feet)

The now and not-yet kingdom:

The kingdom of God is now:

- Luke 17:21; also all of the above words and deeds of Jesus

The kingdom of God is not yet:

- Matthew 22:1–14 (parable of the future wedding feast)
- Luke 19 (parable of the ten minas)
- Revelation 11:15; 21:3–4 (picture of future fulfillment)
- Tension within Scripture: 2 Corinthians 6:4–13 (Paul was in the same position we are!)

Discussion Questions:

- In light of this whole discussion, what do you now understand the phrase "kingdom of God" to mean? Has your definition changed after reading this storyline?
- Is God's kingdom around you? If so, where?
- What does it mean for us today to be citizens of that kingdom? How does this citizenship change our relationship with Jesus and our relationship with the world?

5

The Salvation Storyline

It was dark, raining, and their thin prison uniforms were soaked through. The wind howled around the courtyard as the men stood bleary-eyed and fearful, fighting to keep themselves both as warm and as invisible as they could. They sensed it was serious. The guards had viciously dragged them out of bed in the early hours of the morning and were searching through their cells. They seemed unusually angry.

It wasn't long before the search party returned to join those who had been flashing lights and pointing guns in the terrified prisoners' faces. A brief muttering was followed by the voice of the furious sergeant; rising above the elements, he cried, "Someone here has stolen the guards' rations; if that person does not own up, then none of you, hear me now, none of you, will live to see another sunrise!" The prisoners started shuffling, looking away, looking at their feet, looking anywhere but at the guards. Time seemed to slow. The wind blew, the rain fell, and the dogs growled menacingly. No one spoke.

"You have three minutes," said the sergeant, his voice no longer bellowing but cold, calm, and emotionless. He and his men lowered and readied their weapons. The prisoners started panicking now. "Whoever it was, own up—please own up!" one started screaming.

"Please, I have a family," wept another. Others just knelt, preparing themselves for the inevitable. "Two minutes!" Out from the group a man stepped; he looked just like all the others: scrawny, soaked to the skin, scared, and helpless. He said only three simple words: "It was me."

Bang! The sergeant barely blinked as the man's lifeless body collapsed into the mud. "Let that be a lesson. Back in the cells!" The prisoners, some struggling to register they were still alive, made their way back to the concrete floors on which they slept. The next day's roll call arrived at five thirty a.m.; the prisoners shuffled out. Just as the sergeant was finishing the roll call and the first rays of the sunrise were piercing the clouds, he was informed by a messenger that the man who had owned up had been lying!

"What!" he shouted, red in the face again.

"Wait, sir," said the messenger hurriedly. "The rations hadn't been stolen at all; they'd just been misplaced by the guards."

That man died for nothing, thought the sergeant, disbelievingly.

"That man died for us," marveled the prisoners.

As human beings we are captured by all sorts of stories. One type of story that can particularly stir the emotions, capture our hearts, and bring about a longing to act is an amazing true story of suffering and self-sacrifice. The Bible, without a shadow of a doubt, surpasses any other such story. So it is that we turn to the storyline of salvation. This storyline climaxes when a man is killed on a hill outside Jerusalem, but we must begin in the book of Exodus.

The story of the Exodus of the children of Israel from Egypt has been described as the "controlling narrative" of the entire Bible— basically the story of the Exodus is echoed again and again through the Scriptures. Many of the major stories of the Bible find their beginning in the book of Exodus. When God revealed himself to Moses at the burning bush, he revealed himself first as the God of a people: "I am the God of your father, the God of Abraham, the God of Isaac and the God of Jacob" (Ex. 3:6). He then revealed himself as a God of compassion and of justice: "I have indeed seen the misery of my people in Egypt. I have heard them crying out because of their slave drivers, and I am concerned about their suffering. So I have come down to rescue them ..." (Ex. 3:7–8). God saw the misery of his people, heard their suffering and came to rescue them from slavery. He disarmed Pharaoh and freed his people.

On the night of their salvation from Egypt, the Israelites took part in a special meal: It is called the Passover (Ex. 12). God gave them specific instructions as to what they were to do. The heart of this meal was taking a lamb without any defect, killing this lamb, and smearing the blood on the doorposts of the children of God. Two thousand years later Jesus is described as "our Passover lamb" (1 Cor. 5:7). When the people of Israel smeared the blood on their doorposts, God's judgment (in the form of the Angel of Death) passed over them. When God sees the blood of Jesus on our lives, he passes over us, refusing to judge us as we deserve.

God led the people of Israel to freedom. They passed through the water of the Red Sea and emerged to freedom on the other side (Ex. 14). This is one of the great pictures of baptism; we go down into the water and die to the old life. We rise from the water into a new life of freedom. So the salvation of the people of Israel from slavery in Egypt is itself a picture of the salvation brought about through Jesus.

In Leviticus 16 we read that God starts a really important ceremony called the Day of Atonement. This ceremony was meant to happen once a year. The high priest would kill a bull and a goat and sprinkle their blood in the most holy place. This was the place where God lived and so, apart from this one guy on this one day of the year, no one was allowed in! It was a very special day for God and his people. After this the high priest had to lay his hands on another goat and "confess over it all the wickedness and rebellion of the Israelites—all their sins—and put them on the goat's head" (Lev. 16:21). This goat was then sent off to wander the desert alone. Leviticus teaches that once they did this, they would "be clean from all [their] sins" (v. 30).

If this is what must be done for the forgiveness of sins, why aren't there more lonely goats wandering today's cities and roads?

The answer is in the letter to the Hebrews. It tells us that Jesus is our High Priest and that he doesn't sacrifice goats and bulls, but himself! The Day of Atonement used to happen every year, but Jesus "entered the Most Holy Place once for all by his own blood" (Heb. 9:12). This is exactly what we need!

> *Such a high priest meets our need—one who is holy,*
> *blameless, pure, set apart from sinners, exalted above*
> *the heavens. Unlike the other high priests, he does not*
> *need to offer sacrifices day after day, first for his own*
> *sins, and then for the sins of the people. He sacrificed*
> *for their sins once for all when he offered himself. For*
> *the law appoints as high priests men who are weak;*
> *but the oath, which came after the law, appointed*

the Son, who has been made perfect forever. (Heb.
7:26–28)

This is why, when Jesus died on the cross, the curtain separating the most holy place from the people was torn in two (Luke 23:45). Jesus' death removed the barrier of sin that exists between us and God—something no high priest except God himself could do—and that's why the tear was made from top to bottom.

The theme of God saving his people is present throughout the Old Testament. God saved his people from Egypt. He gave them laws to obey and instructions on what to do if they messed it up. These laws are present throughout the rest of the Old Testament. Israel often got it wrong, but whenever they turned back to God, he forgave them. If we read the books of the Judges, Kings, and Chronicles, we are reading about the history of ancient Israel. In these books Israel's history seems to go around in circles: Israel is in a good place with God; then they sin; then they are conquered by an enemy power; then they repent; then God saves them. The underlying theme of the Exodus is present here, in God intervening to free his people from foreign powers. The same is true of the exile. When Jerusalem falls in 2 Kings 25 and the Jews are taken into exile by Babylon, God promises restoration. Just like the time he rescued them from Egypt, so too he will (and did) rescue them from Babylon.

God saving his people, then, is a theme that runs throughout the Old Testament. It climaxes, however, with the ultimate act of salvation. So it is that in this chapter we will pay special attention to the great symbol of the Christian faith and the amazing means of our salvation ... the cross.

We can't get far as Christians without meeting the cross. We're obsessed with it. Many of our churches not only contain crosses but are built in the shape of the cross. We wear it around our necks; we tattoo it on our arms; and every time we take Communion we're reminding ourselves of the gruesome way in which Jesus died. The gospel writers shared this obsession; a third of the story of Jesus' life is taken up by his death. There's nothing about his teenage years, the bands he liked, the clothes he wore, and whether he had arguments with his mom. Yet for many of us, this central Christian teaching is a stumbling block to the Christian faith; for many of us, the cross raises more questions than it answers.

Was the cross necessary? If so, why? If God really is all-loving and all-powerful, why couldn't he just forgive us anyway? Where's the "justice" in God punishing his innocent Son? Did it have to be Jesus? Doesn't it seem slightly weird and cultish that when we come to church we're eating and drinking the "body and blood of Jesus"? What's it all got to do with the forgiveness of sins anyway?

Before we look at these questions, let's look at the event itself....

The Gospels tell us a lot about the days leading up to the cross: We read how Jesus kept telling his disciples he had to, and was going to, die; we learn how he was betrayed by a friend he loved and sold for the going rate of a slave; we're told about the terrible agony of Jesus in Gethsemane while his disciples, his closest friends, fell asleep on him three times.

At one point Jesus is described as sweating blood. During World War II, the Nazis carried out torture experiments and found if you terrified someone enough, it was possible to make them sweat blood. After his arrest Jesus was accused by religious leaders and proclaimed innocent by the Roman governor Pilate three times. Eventually Pilate gave in to the will of the people. Jesus had a "crown" of thorns rammed onto his scalp, the aim of which was not just to inflict great pain, but also to humiliate the man who claimed to be King of the Jews. He was stripped and then whipped until there was no skin left on his back. All the while he was being screamed at, punched, and spat on. Then they loaded the cross onto his raw, bleeding back and made him carry it till he collapsed from exhaustion. At this point all the gospel writers simply say, "They crucified him."

Two thousand years later it's difficult for us to grasp the sheer horror of what happened; the cross has, for many, become a mere fashion accessory. We can fill in what the Gospels leave out from historical accounts of the time. Crucifixion was the method of execution used for common slaves, not Roman citizens; it was not only excruciatingly painful but also incredibly humiliating. They would nail the victim by his wrists and feet to the cross, leaving him completely naked and stripped of dignity. The person would be in complete agony and total shame. Sometimes death would take days, the victim dehydrating during the burning heat of the day and shivering during the cold of the night.

Most would die a drawn-out death from suffocation. The nails through the wrists would cause the victim to hang in such a way that pressure on the lungs made breathing near impossible. To breathe, the victim would be forced to physically lift himself up. Pushing down on the nails in his feet and pulling up by the nails through his wrists, his shredded back would scrape against splintered wood. Suffocation would claim the victims when their strength to lift themselves was exhausted. The soldiers would speed this process up by breaking the legs (which would mean the victim would be unable to push themselves up to breathe). When the soldiers came to break Jesus' legs, they found he was already dead.

We know what happened. Why did it happen?

On a purely human level it's not difficult to pick out the reasons for Jesus' crucifixion. Jesus was born into an Israel dominated by oppressive Roman rule and governed by paranoid, power-hungry, competitive religious and political leaders. Jesus' popularity with the people, combined with his controversial teaching and actions, such as healing on the Sabbath, challenged their authority. The Gospels depict Judas betraying him out of greed, the priests accusing him out of indignation and envy, and Pilate sentencing him out of cowardice. Yet this is only part of the story; scratch beneath the surface, and something much deeper was going on. The cross was planned by God, executed by God, and finished by God. It was as if God the Father said to God the Son, "Your mission, should you choose to accept it, is to become one of them; to die on the cross; to take their sin, guilt, and shame on yourself; and to bring them home." Jesus—and this is important—chose the cross; it was not imposed on him by Pontius Pilate or by his Father.

Why Is the Cross Necessary?

We were created for relationship with God—an amazing, loving relationship of dependence on God. We were also made to have loving, interdependent relationships with each other. We the human race, however, chose not to fulfill this purpose for which we were made. We chose to make up purposes of our own. The primary use of the word *sin* in the Bible refers not to "breaking the rules" but rather to "missing the mark." The first sin the human race committed was choosing independence from God, choosing our own way. This is represented in the book of Genesis, where Adam and Eve deliberately go against God's command. This first sin of the human race is referred to as "the fall." The fall was essentially humanity missing the mark, missing the purpose for which we were created. Murder, anger, adultery, theft, greed, war, and other examples of "rule breaking" are simply the consequences of our missing the mark. Sin is spelled s-i-n; the heart of sin is "I"—putting "I" first.

How Did Our Sin Affect God?

In order to answer the question, we need to look at what God is like. The Bible tells us very clearly in signs, images, and stories that God is holy. We learn that God is utterly pure and as a result, because of his very nature, demands perfect justice. In short—God is holy and can't stand to be near our sin.

And yet the Bible also tells us that God is love. What do we mean when we say "God is love"? If God is love, we can paraphrase the famous passage on love of 1 Corinthians 13 by swapping the word *God* for *love;* it then reads:

> *God is patient, God is kind. God does not envy, God does not boast, God is not proud. God is not rude, God is not self-seeking, God is not easily angered, God keeps no record of wrongs. God does not delight in evil but rejoices with the truth. God always protects, always trusts, always hopes, always perseveres. God never fails. (vv. 4–8, paraphrased)*

We might be sinners, but God loves us!

So we have a tension in the Bible created by our sin: Because of his holiness God cannot bear to look at us; but because of his love God cannot bear to look away from us.

How Does Our Sin Affect Us?

Our sin traps us and blinds us to who God is. In biblical times, slavery was common. A slave had no rights and was owned by another, meaning he or she was at the mercy of the owner. When the Bible tells us we are slaves to sin, this is the imagery it's using. We all have friends or family who have addictions, whether to drinking, smoking, gambling, drugs, eating disorders, sex, or whatever. If we're honest with ourselves, however, we all have become slaves to what we call sin. That which we thought we could enjoy a little bit of ends up owning us. For many of us Paul's problem in Romans 7 is our own:

> ... *sold as a slave to sin. I do not understand what I do. For what I want to do I do not do, but what I hate I do.... For I have the desire to do what is good, but I cannot carry it out. For what I do is not the good I want to do; no, the evil I do not want to do —this I keep on doing.* (vv. 14–15, 18–19)

It is clear that as a human race we have been quicker to listen to the voice of Satan than the voice of God, quicker to follow the temptations of Satan than the commands of God. Satan was instrumental in the fall of the human race. The Bible teaches that Satan tempts human beings, accuses us, and undermines our relationship with God.

So, having looked at the problems that sin raises both for God and for ourselves, why is the cross the only solution? The Bible gives more than one answer to this question; it presents us with different "windows" on the cross, and there are different ways of understanding this one event. If we don't look through the different windows, we'll miss the full picture.

The Cross as Penal Substitution

The theological phrase for the first window is "penal substitution." This phrase is taken from the picture of the law courts. "Penal" comes from "penalty," so "penal substitution" means a substitute paying the penalty, taking the punishment, in the place of the one who received the sentence. The key scripture for this picture is the amazing passage in Isaiah 53, which is an Old Testament prophecy about Jesus:

> *Surely he took up our infirmities and carried our sorrows, yet we considered him stricken by God, smitten by him, and afflicted. But he was pierced for our transgressions, he was crushed for our iniquities; the punishment that brought us peace was upon him, and by his wounds we are healed. We all, like sheep, have gone astray, each of us has turned to his own way; and the LORD has laid on him the iniquity of us all. (vv. 4–6)*

We mentioned earlier that half of the problem for God is that he cannot bear to look at us because of our filth (one of the biblical words for sin). Because of his holiness and requirement for justice,

God cannot ignore sin, and Romans 6:23 tells us that "the wages of sin is death." The other half of the problem is that God cannot bear to look away from us because of his love. God can't ignore sin and he won't ignore us! The cross is the place where God's love and justice meet.

How Is God's Love Shown through the Cross?

It was God on the cross. He didn't open a window in heaven and shout down, "I love you." He didn't send a messenger, a servant, or a colleague. He came himself. God's love is shown through God himself dying a horrific death on the cross. Someone had to receive justice for our sin; God himself chose to be that someone. Actions speak louder than words. This perfect act was an act of perfect love.

How Is God's Holiness and Justice Satisfied through the Cross?

It was the human race who sinned, and so the human race had to pay the penalty demanded by God's justice. If someone is in debt to the bank, they need someone in credit to cancel that debt. The entire human race, however, was sinful. We were all in debt. God became a human being. And more than that, he became the only righteous human being, the only human being with credit. As a result God as a human was able to pay the debt of the entire human race.

Jesus was the only one who could die on the cross because as both God and man, he could display the love of God the same time as paying the penalty for humanity. God's demand for justice is satisfied on the cross (in what happened to Jesus), and God's longing to love is satisfied (in that God himself was on the cross). Christ on the cross is the only solution to the dilemma of God's holiness and love. Romans 3:26 says of God and the cross: "He did it to demonstrate his justice at the present time, so as to be just and the one who justifies." God is holy and therefore is justice. God is love, and so he is the one who justifies.

Popular speaker and evangelist J. John tells the story of a bus driver taking a group of school children on a trip. The bus is going downhill on winding lanes. Suddenly the brakes fail. The driver sees a field at the bottom of the hill and knows that if he can manage to steer the bus into that field, it will come to a gradual halt and disaster will be avoided. The difficulty is that as he nears the field he sees, very clearly, a little boy playing in the gate! The driver knows that if he goes into the field, he will kill the boy, but that if he doesn't, all the children on the bus will almost certainly die. He chooses the field. The children are saved but the little boy is killed.

Later the parents of the survivors look for the driver to thank him. One approaches a policeman saying, "Where is the driver? I must thank him!"

The policeman replies, "He's in deep mourning. On the way into the field, he ran over a little boy."

"Oh!" exclaims the parent.

"Yes." The policeman nods sadly. "And what's more, the boy he killed was his own son."

Human pictures are sometimes the best we have to illustrate divine truth. This story illustrates in stark terms the sacrifice God made on the cross. However, as with all human pictures about God, there are limitations. The major limitation of our story is that it can suggest that God killed his innocent Son who was unaware and had no say in the matter. We have already recognized that Jesus was not a helpless little boy; he deliberately chose the cross, knowing what it would involve. What our story does illustrate is the agony and suffering of the Father, knowing there was no other way to save us than for his Son to die a painful death. The nails of the cross truly pierced the heart of the Trinity. Penal substitution then—God taking the penalty in the place of humanity—is one insight into the reasons for the cross.

The Cross as Reconciliation

Another window on the cross is that of reconciliation. In any relationship, if there's a falling out, somebody has to make peace. Imagine if there's a problem because one person lied, cheated, betrayed, and dishonored the other. You would expect the one at fault to be the one who has to make amends. Not so with God. He, the wronged party, came to draw us together with him by making peace. Just as Jesus in his body, fully God and fully human, unites God and man, so Jesus in his actions on the cross brings together God and the human race. Dying on the cross, Jesus prays, "Father, forgive them, for they do not know what they are doing" (Luke 23:34). Even while we were putting him to death, Jesus was representing us to God and God to us. When God looks at the cross, he sees our representative. Prayer has been described as "standing in the gap" between sinful humanity and a holy God. Jesus' prayer on the cross didn't just stand in the gap; it bridged the gap. Through his death on the cross, Jesus united God and humanity. The falling out in the relationship is dealt with and, wonderfully, we are reconciled to God. We get to share once again in joyful nearness, closeness, and intimacy with God.

All this is from God, who reconciled us to himself through Christ and gave us the ministry of reconciliation: that God was reconciling the world to himself in Christ, not counting men's sins against them. And he has committed to us the message of reconciliation. (2 Cor. 5:18–19)

On the cross Jesus not only opened the way for humanity to be reconciled to God, he also made it possible for us to be reconciled to one another. We find the picture of this in John where Jesus looks down from the cross and says to his mother: "Dear woman, here is your son," and to John, "Here is your mother" (John 19:26–27). Even on the cross Jesus was uniting people: "From that time on, this disciple took her into his home" (v. 27). The Bible tells us we are one in Christ; it's through Jesus' death on the cross that we are reconciled to each other.

Almost every day we read or hear on the news about the tension, conflict, and hatred that exists in the Middle East between the Jews and the Arabs, particularly in Israel. Mike and I attended a Christian event there recently. At this event there were both Jewish Christians and Arab Christians. Each night someone would tell the story of how they became a Christian. One night a young Arab woman stood up and told her testimony. She had grown up in a Muslim family in the West Bank and, in her words, had "nothing but hatred for Jews" (remarkably she was explaining this in a room full of Jewish Christians). One day a Christian visited her parents' house and talked with her family. The result of this was that her family became Christians. When she found out her parents had become Christians, this woman became tremendously angry; she was a very devout Muslim. She told us that she was full of hate. It got to the point where she went to the terrorist group Hamas and had discussions about becoming a suicide bomber; she wanted to take as many Jews with her as possible.

Shortly after this she was diagnosed with a rare cancer of the blood and became very scared. A friend suggested she pray to Jesus to heal her. The woman said she couldn't pray to Jesus. The friend then suggested she pray to "the God who made her." The woman agreed. She prayed that whoever the God who created her was, whether the God of Muhammad or the God of Jesus, that he would come and heal her. That night she had a vision of Jesus, and when she woke the next day, she was miraculously healed! The person interviewing her asked how she felt about the Jewish people since she'd become a Christian. This woman of around twenty, who had been so full of hate, looked out at the crowd of Jews and Arabs and said, "Now I have nothing but love for them."

It is because Jesus first loved us that we are able to love others as he does. This is a love that overcomes all barriers and heals all wounds. It is a love that focuses not just on our friends but on our enemies as well. It is the love that Jesus displayed as he died for the people who were putting him to death. The cross reconciles us to God, and through the power of the cross we can be truly and deeply reconciled to each other. The only permanent solution for a constantly warring humanity is found not in military strength, not in alliances, not in the nuclear deterrent, and not even in the United Nations. The only permanent hope is the gospel of Jesus Christ.

The Cross as Redemption

Another key word used to describe what Jesus did on the cross is *redemption*. To look through this window, we need to understand the practice of slavery in biblical times. The buying and selling of slaves was common practice. It was possible for someone to pay a "ransom" in order to redeem a slave completely and set him free. Talking of slavery in our twenty-first-century world can almost seem quite alien and strange, a concept or idea we've heard about but never actually experienced. This would not have been the case when the New Testament writers used this imagery. Slavery was a harsh and concrete reality in the world around. It was literally a bondage from which you could not escape unless someone paid the ransom. What's more, freedom for a slave would have been an amazing gift. When the New Testament speaks of Jesus dying as a "ransom for many" and bringing about our "redemption," it is pointing to the cross as the answer to our slavery to sin. On the cross Jesus pays the price and sets us free.

Let's try and come up with a twenty-first-century picture for this image of Jesus ransoming us. Imagine Jesus walking into the cosmic superstore and grabbing a basket. Heading down an aisle, he sees on the shelf a "Ben," and he puts him in the basket; then he sees a "Rachel" and sticks her in the basket; next he sees a "Tom" … and so on. By the time he gets to the check out, he's cleared the whole shop! The cashier says, "This is going to be very expensive. How are you going to pay for it all? Visa, MasterCard, or cash?" The intensely biblical point of this rather lame illustration is that Jesus gets into the cash register himself. He pays for us with himself. It's not cheap. It costs him everything. He redeems us with his own blood. The result of this is not just that we are freed slaves—it's so much more amazing! God values us so much, so deeply, that he has redeemed us from slavery and adopted us as his very own children!

John marvels, "How great is the love the Father has lavished on us, that we should be called children of God! And that is what we are!" (1 John 3:1).

The Cross as Victory

Christus Victor is the theological phrase to describe our next view of the cross. You probably guessed that its literal meaning is "Christ Victorious," referring to the victory that Christ won over sin, death, and Satan on the cross. When we think of victory, we think about strength, power, and domination. Jesus redefined victory. He won not by becoming stronger but by, on the cross, becoming weaker. He allowed Satan and us to do our worst to him. While Satan thought that the cross was his greatest triumph, it turned out to be his ultimate defeat.

The victory of Satan lies in the fact that when he says "you are not worthy" to sinful humanity, he's right. We are not worthy, we are guilty, we are sinful. The victory of Christ on the cross, however, is that we are made worthy. Jesus has taken all our sin, guilt, and shame on himself.

It has no hold over us. We are freed through his victory on the cross. So now when Satan accuses us, we don't plead our goodness but the righteousness of Jesus.

Jesus, referring to Satan, says, "The thief comes only to steal and kill and destroy; I have come that they may have life, and have it to the full" (John 10:10). Satan's major aim was to separate us from God and to kill us by separating us from eternal life. Having suffered both sin and death, Jesus rose again to life! The resurrection of Jesus broke the power of death. Through his death and resurrection, Jesus won for us a relationship with God that will last for eternity. Jesus' final cry on the cross was, "It is finished" (John 19:30). It is over; Satan has been disarmed and defeated. "And having disarmed the powers and authorities, he made a public spectacle of them, triumphing over them by the cross" (Col. 2:15).

I recently spent some time trying to understand the cross—but felt as though I just didn't get it. At the time, I wrote this:

> Recently I went to hear a talk. It was nothing to do with the cross, but as I watched the preacher, I could almost feel the joy pouring out of him. At one point someone asked him, "Do you find it difficult to believe?" His response was, "For me, belief is risk. But I'm a captive of hope, I'm a prisoner of a God who stopped me in my tracks, embraced me, and kissed me." I thought, "Wow!" I wandered home that night thinking how much I'd love to be a captive of hope and a prisoner of a God who stopped me in my tracks, embraced me, and kissed me! The next day I was reading a book (*Instrument of Thy Peace* by Alan Paton), and he wrote, "I should like to write a few words for those who have repented and who have been forgiven (whether in private or public confession, or by the person they have harmed), but who still cannot feel forgiven …" As I read this, I thought, *Perfect, that's exactly where I'm at.* I was expecting the author to go on and reassure me that I was completely forgiven, that

it had all been finished on the cross, and that even though I hadn't really accepted that I was forgiven I should stop worrying. Instead the very next line read: "There is something wrong with you. You are literally not understanding the gospel."

I did a complete double take! What did he mean, I wasn't understanding the gospel?! Of course I understand it. I've been a Christian for years! But the more I thought about it, the more I started to agree with him.

Above we've outlined some of the pictures of the cross, and hopefully we've done it in a clear way to help you understand the cross in your *head*. But what I've been learning in a very real way is that the death and resurrection of Jesus has to grow in meaning in your *heart*. This is where I went wrong. Mike and I have a friend who is a very bald preacher. He used to say that the reason he's got no hair is because God is constantly banging him on the head—God is trying to get what's in his head down into his heart. This can sometimes be the biggest eighteen inches in the world. I have a friend who meditates on the cross each day; she'll sit and write on a piece of paper what the cross means to her. She is the best evangelist I know. Why? Because she knows what the cross means to her and to others. The point of understanding the cross is not to be a better evangelist, it is to know the truth which sets us free (John 8:32). If we actually "get it," then nothing can stand against that; it will bring the freedom, joy, and hope the preacher mentioned earlier.

Although we've focused on the cross throughout this chapter, it cannot be understood without the resurrection. For two weeks before Easter, I was reading just the crucifixion account and stopping at the death of Jesus. By the time Easter day came, I was literally desperate to read the account of the resurrection. The hope of the cross stems from the fact that there is life after death. The good news of the cross is only good because Jesus rose again. I'm still a long way from understanding deep in my heart what the death and resurrection mean, but I'm not going to stop seeking that understanding. Since I've started, I've grown in knowing in my heart that I'm forgiven and knowing the goodness of my God more and more in everyday life.

This chapter began by recognizing that as human beings we are captured by all sorts of stories; we want to finish it by pointing out that as human beings we are freed by only one story. This story is the true story of the Bible, and it is a story of salvation. The pattern is set in the book of Exodus and continues throughout Scripture. God is constantly intervening to save his people in all sorts of ways. God's plan of salvation, a plan that kicked in from the moment of creation, climaxed with a man dying on a cross outside a city called Jerusalem.

On that cross God himself displayed his justice and love through suffering on our behalf. He reconciled the world to himself, restoring us to deep and intimate relationship with him. He redeemed us to the point where we go from being slaves to sin to being children of God. And he won a victory that we could never win for ourselves. He finished it. He defeated sin and he conquered death; he did it out of love for us, and he longs for us to share in this victory. Without the cross and resurrection of Christ, there could be no salvation.

For many people the cross seems bizarre, medieval, and foolish; this has always been the case. Paul says:

> *Jews demand miraculous signs and Greeks look for wisdom, but we preach Christ crucified: a stumbling block to Jews and foolishness to Gentiles, but to those whom God has called, both Jews and Greeks, Christ the power of God and the wisdom of God. (1 Cor. 1:22–24)*

The center of our faith is a truth that is difficult to grasp precisely because it is the opposite of the wisdom of the world. Nevertheless this glorious truth of salvation is something to be embraced, savored, trusted, and rejoiced over. There was no other way; it is the choice, the wisdom, and the love of God. It becomes powerful and effective over our lives when we respond to its message of the love, justice, and salvation of God. It is for this reason that Paul declares, "For I resolved to know nothing while I was with you except Jesus Christ and him crucified" (1 Cor. 2:2).

Salvation Storyline Paperchase:

Salvation is a recurring theme throughout the Bible:

- Exodus 12; compare 1 Corinthians 5:7 (Passover)
- Exodus 14; compare John 3 (baptism)
- Leviticus 16; compare Hebrews 9 (atonement)

(We see cycles of the Exodus repeated throughout Israel's history, though it is difficult to give any one reference for this.)

The event of the cross:
- Matthew 27:32–56
- Mark 15:21–32
- Luke 23:26–49
- John 19:18–37

(Again, it is difficult to give any one reference for these pictures, but below are a few foundational verses.)

The meaning of the cross:
- Isaiah 53; Hebrews 7—10 (penal substitution)
- Luke 23:34; 2 Corinthians 5:18–19; Romans 5:9–11 (reconciliation)
- Matthew 20:28; Galatians 3:26–4:7 (redemption)
- John 19:30; Colossians 2:15 (Christ victorious). Not forgetting here the resurrection—see Matthew 28; Mark 16; Luke 24; John 20—21.
- 1 Corinthians 1:22–24; 2:2 (the cross seems foolish but is central)

Discussion Questions:

- Which window of the cross speaks to you the most? Why do you think that is?
- Is salvation mainly something you understand in your head or your heart? Why?
- If you had to express to someone why you need salvation and what difference it has made to your life (and you weren't allowed to use Christian jargon), what would you say?
- What does the cross mean to you? Write it down, if possible.

6

The Worship Storyline

Worship music has become a multimillion-dollar business. Some worship albums sell hundreds of thousands of copies around the world, and some worship leaders are in danger of becoming the latest Christian celebrities. This has caused a conflict. Traditional church music vies with contemporary rock tunes, and purists feel worship has been spoiled by commercialization. In this context let's turn to look at what the Bible says worship is about and trace this golden thread that runs from Genesis to Revelation.

In the beginning God created the human race for a purpose. That purpose was that we would live in relationship with him. The relationship was intended to be defined by mutual love. Worship can be defined as the expression and outworking of our love for God. This means more than just singing songs!

Imagine a couple in love. If the two of them "expressed and outworked" their love for each other through kissing, making out, kissing, and a bit more making out, then it could be said to be a tiny bit shallow! If, on the other hand, they were constantly texting and phoning each other, spent hours in conversation with each other, were always trying to do things to please each other, and were incredibly faithful to each

other, then we could say their love has a lot more depth. Worship is the
expression and outworking of our love for God. For our love to have
depth, our worship must be more than just singing songs—the spiritual equivalent of kissing. This is not to say kissing is not important.
Kissing and intimacy are important in a relationship—very important!
At the same time, our worship, the expression of our love for God, is
outworked through the whole of our lives. Our lives are to be lived in
this mutual, loving relationship with God.

What Do We Worship?

Let's begin to trace the storyline. God told Adam and Eve they could
enjoy all that paradise had to offer with the exception of one tree, on
which grew the fruit of the knowledge of good and evil. They took
this fruit. As a result they began to hide from God and from one
another. The heart of their sin was in choosing to turn from worship
of God the Creator to worship of the creation. Maybe Adam and
Eve thought they could have the fruit *and* worship God; the fact is,
as soon as they ate the fruit, they hid from God. You cannot worship
God and creation: It is one or the other.

The biblical word for choosing to worship creation is *idolatry,*
and this is the most common theme in the entire Old Testament.
Indeed, the Bible makes clear that the greatest issue facing people is
not whether we worship, because every human being is a worshipper. It has never been a choice between the worship of God or the
worship of nothing; it's always God versus idols. Those who don't
believe in God sometimes look down on those who "worship"; they
sometimes pride themselves on the fact they don't worship anything.
But to be a human is to be a worshipper.

When we stop worshipping God, we don't worship nothing; we worship anything: The question is not whether we will worship, but who or what we will worship. We can read the pages of the Old Testament and feel smugly superior as we see the people worshipping things they've made—bits of wood instead of the Creator of the universe. The fact is, we haven't "advanced" as far as we sometimes think. Some of us have swapped the worship of gods called "Baal" for the worship of gods called "celebrities." Instead of sacrificing to gain the favor of pieces of wood, we're now willing to pay the designer price that will earn us the approval of those around us. Instead of listening at the shrines for the latest prophecies, many of us listen to the utterances of Oprah. Given that worship can be defined as the expression and outworking of our love for God, it is fair to say that as the human race we spend most of our time expressing and outworking our love for (worshipping) money, sex, fame, power, celebrity, each other, ourselves … to name but a few.

Israel's Worship

God's response to humanity's insistence on worshipping creation was given in Deuteronomy 6:5. He told the people of Israel, "Love the LORD your God with all your heart and with all your soul and with all your strength." The foundation of Israel's law was not a dry obedience to God but a life lived out of love for God. It's the difference between being a slave and being a lover: If you're a slave, you do it because you have to; if you're a lover, you do it because you want to. Both might get the job done, but they are worlds apart. Worship is the expression of Israel's love for God.

For many people Leviticus is the hardest book in the Bible to read. It's the instruction manual for Israel's worship. There are instructions on what to wear and how much incense to throw around, but right at the heart of it all, God says, "Offer sacrifices." Worship was the heart of Israel's life, and sacrifice was at the heart of Israel's worship. During every temple meeting, sacrifices were made. Sometimes it was an animal, sometimes it was grain, but every time, it went up in smoke. They were offering tokens of creation, and by sacrificing them to God, they were saying every time they worshipped, "You, the Creator, are more important than creation."

Let's go back to our illustration of our couple in love ... we'll call them Joel and Ali. (And we are aware that this is not the perfect illustration—God is not our boyfriend or girlfriend!) Joel wants to show Ali she matters to him more than his salary. What does he do? He spends a fortune on her—he buys her flowers, takes her out for meals, pays for her hair appointments, and sends her expensive gifts. What Ali hears from all of this is that Joel would be willing to give anything, to spend anything; all that he has is hers! What Joel wants to say to Ali is, "Ali, you are more important to me than everything I have." To express this, he sacrifices; to show Ali she matters to him more than money, he spends money on her!

What the Israelites were saying when they worshipped God was, "God, you are more important than everything we have." Each sacrifice represented the best of creation being given up as a token of love for the Creator. One of the things Israel was doing when they sacrificed was reversing the idolatry of humanity.

Despite what they were instructed to do, the people of Israel, even before they entered the Promised Land, messed it up. In Exodus

32, while Moses was up on the mountain having an amazing face-to-face encounter with God and receiving the Ten Commandments, Aaron and the people of Israel were busy making a golden calf to worship down below. God knew that the golden calf was not a one-off occurrence, and said to Moses before he died:

> *You are going to rest with your fathers, and these people will soon prostitute themselves to the foreign gods of the land they are entering. They will forsake me and break the covenant I made with them. (Deut. 31:16)*

Just before Joshua died, when the people were settling down in the Promised Land, he said to them:

> *You are not able to serve the LORD. He is a holy God; he is a jealous God. He will not forgive your rebellion and your sins. If you forsake the LORD and serve foreign gods, he will turn and bring disaster on you and make an end of you, after he has been good to you. (Josh. 24:19–20)*

The big issue about idolatry is not that it breaks God's laws but that it breaks relationship with God. God is a jealous God. His jealousy is not the petty jealousy of someone who doesn't have the latest mobile phone; it's the jealousy of a husband whose wife is having an affair. Idolatry is adultery.

All the Old Testament prophets told Israel, again and again, "You're messing it up; turn back to the God who loves you!" The problem was that even when they did sacrifice, they never managed to love God with their whole hearts. It wouldn't matter if Joel bought Ali flowers every day if at the same time he was having an affair with the girl down the road. Israel's sacrifices, even if they made them all day every day, would mean nothing to God until they were faithful to him. After all, who wants to share a lover? Even David, the hero of Israel, the guy who wrote half the Psalms and who offered thousands of sacrifices to God, committed adultery. The problem was not the sacrifices; the problem was Israel. What God was looking for was not perfect sacrifices but perfect worshippers.

Jesus' Worship

God looked all over the earth for one human being who would offer him perfect worship because he or she was a perfect worshipper. He could not find one until … Jesus.

Jesus lived a perfect life. The point the Gospels make is that he was the only one. Jesus had twelve disciples. We know Judas gets bad press—he betrayed Jesus. What about the other eleven? How did they do? Actually not a lot better. In the garden of Gethsemane, when Jesus' soul was in agony, the disciples managed to fall asleep three times. Why did Matthew want us to know that the disciples fell asleep three times? Once could be excused as weakness. Twice isn't great. Three times suggests they were pretty useless.

It's the same with old Peter—"the rock"—the man on whom Jesus was going to build his church. He managed to deny Jesus three times. On the third occasion Matthew even records that "he began to call down curses on himself and he swore to them, 'I don't know the man!'" (Matt. 26:74). In other words it's as if Peter said, "Watch my lips! I've never met him, I don't know him, and if I'm lying, may God strike me dead!" Matthew goes out of his way to make his point. When it came to the crunch, when the rubber hit the road, when it came to the cross, everyone, including his closest friends, let Jesus down. When Jesus went to the cross, what did the disciples, his closest companions for the last three years, the men whose feet he had knelt and washed, do to help him? A word of encouragement? An expression of trust or understanding? They betrayed him, they fell asleep on him, and they denied him. What he did on the cross, Jesus did all on his own. And what did he do on the cross? He offered an act of perfect worship to his Father.

Let's connect the dots. Hebrews 10:12 describes Jesus' work on the cross as offering "for all time one sacrifice for sins." For Israel sacrifice was worship, so what our modern prayer books call the "one perfect sacrifice" was the "one perfect worship." In Jesus, God found a perfect worshipper. He never sinned. In other words he loved God perfectly and this love was expressed through the whole of the way he lived his life. Jesus' motivation for living was to please his Father. In John 4:34, speaking to his disciples, Jesus said, "My food … is to do the will of him who sent me and to finish his work." Later, in John 5:30, Jesus says, "By myself I can do nothing; I judge only as I hear, and my judgment is just, for I seek not to please myself but him who sent me."

Jesus was the only human being in history who loved God with all his heart, all his soul, and all his strength. His love, his worship, was perfect. The whole of his life was lived in perfect obedience to God—this is why when it came to the ultimate sacrifice, the cross, he was the "one perfect sacrifice." In his death Jesus didn't just choose the Creator over tokens of creation: He chose the Creator over life itself. To quote Martyn Layzell's song: "You chose the cross with every breath, the perfect life, the perfect death, you chose the cross …"[2]

The one perfect sacrifice by the one perfect worshipper is the one perfect worship. What is our response to this? The song continues, "I'm lost in wonder, I'm lost in love, I'm lost in praise forevermore …"

Every second Jesus lived, and every moment of his death, was an act of perfect worship to God. Wow!

Our Worship

So how do we worship now? Do we need to sacrifice? We don't need to sacrifice in order to make up for sin, as we have seen Jesus' sacrifice was "once for all." Is there still a place for sacrifice in worship? Absolutely! So is it the iPod? Should we burn our clothes? How about slashing our tires? Well, actually it's so much more: "Therefore, I urge you, brothers, in view of God's mercy, to offer your bodies as living sacrifices, holy and pleasing to God—this is your spiritual act of worship" (Rom. 12:1). We are told that, in response to the wonder and mercy of God, we are to give him all that we are. We are to worship with all that we do. Not to earn love from God, but because of God's love for us.

Today lots of us make the mistake of thinking worship entails singing songs and what we do at church. For the people of Israel, worship was so much more than singing songs; it was a way of life. For Jesus it was all of his life. So for us, in response to God's mercies, it should involve all that we think and say and do. At the same time, we mustn't downgrade what we do when we're at church or what we do when we sing to God. Worship, as well as involving the whole of life, is about specific acts of devotion! If it wasn't, the Bible would not repeatedly say of Israel at specific occasions, "They worshipped."

In 2 Chronicles chapter 7, when Solomon dedicated the temple, "… they worshiped" (v. 3). This involved the sacrifice of 22,000 cattle and 120,000 sheep and goats (v. 5). But it also involved singing, "He is good; his love endures forever" (v. 3). When the Magi came to the stable, "they bowed down and worshiped him" (Matt. 2:11). After Jesus rose from the dead, "When they [the disciples] saw him, they worshiped him" (Matt. 28:17). In Revelation 4 and 5, we read that the four living creatures, the twenty-four elders, ten thousand times ten thousand angels, and the whole of creation will worship.

One Greek word for worship commonly used in the Bible is *latreo*. It literally means "to serve," and to worship is to serve him with the whole of our lives. Another is *proskuneo*; this is the most common word for worship in the Bible and means "to come toward, to kiss." To worship him is to bow before him and kiss the hem of his garment at specific times in specific places. Specific acts of devotion are like the kiss in a marriage.

What does worship as specific acts of devotion look like? Worship is a physical activity! In the Bible it involves singing, clapping, dancing, lifting the eyes, lifting the head, lifting the hands, standing, kneeling, falling face down, and wearing sackcloth and ashes. Oddly enough it rarely involves just sitting! Let's look at a few examples of this in the storyline of worship through Scripture.

The first example of singing comes in Exodus 15 after Israel has been freed from slavery and escaped through the Red Sea. Salvation and singing go hand in hand! The first declaration by Israel that the Lord is King comes in song. Moses, Miriam, and all the Israelites sang:

> "I will sing to the LORD, for he is highly exalted ... The LORD is my strength and my song; he has become my salvation. He is my God, and I will praise him, my father's God, and I will exalt him ... the LORD will reign forever and ever" ... Then Miriam the prophetess, Aaron's sister, took a tambourine in her hand, and all the women followed her, with tambourines and dancing. (Ex. 15:1–2, 18, 20)

Israel's new life with God began with singing, music, and dancing. During the highpoints of Israel's life, they also sang, and the Psalms are full of commands and encouragements to sing and make music to the Lord:

> Sing for joy to God our strength; shout aloud to the God of Jacob! Begin the music, strike the tambourine, play the melodious harp and lyre. (Ps. 81:1–2)

> Sing to the LORD a new song, his praise in the assembly of the saints. Let Israel rejoice in their Maker; let the people of Zion be glad in their King. Let them praise his name with dancing and make music to him with tambourine and harp. For the LORD takes delight in

his people; he crowns the humble with salvation. Let
the saints rejoice in this honor and sing for joy on
their beds. (Ps. 149:1–5)

From just two psalms we see we're commanded to sing, shout, make music, dance, hit a tambourine, play the harp and lyre, and even to sing for joy on our beds! There are loads of encouragements like this all the way through the Psalms. (Look for yourself at Psalm 30:4; 47:6; 66:1–2; and many others.) Singing is worship, and there's meant to be an element of celebration, of party.

The New Testament doesn't give us a blueprint for how we're meant to worship. Nowhere does it say what the sound levels should be like and how long the prayers are allowed to be. In Ephesians we're told to "not get drunk on wine, which leads to debauchery. Instead, be filled with the Spirit. Speak to one another with psalms, hymns and spiritual songs. Sing and make music in your heart to the Lord, always giving thanks to God the Father for everything, in the name of our Lord Jesus Christ" (vv. 5:18–20).

This echoes the principles we read in the Old Testament: We're to sing, make music in our hearts as well as with our lips, and always give thanks!

What is it that motivates us to worship like this? It is surely our response of gratitude for who God is and all he has done for us.

Perhaps the greatest picture of worship in the entire Bible can be found in Revelation chapters 4 and 5. Here we see a snapshot of the worship of heaven. It is quite colorful and one impressive light and sound show! There's thunder and lightning, rainbows and emeralds, lamps blazing, elders throwing their crowns down, ten thousand times ten thousand angels, and the whole of creation. If our major lesson from this is simply that the worship of heaven is creative and colorful, we'd be missing the point. All of this only makes sense when we are introduced to the star of the show, the object and reason for our worship: "Then I saw a Lamb, looking as if it had been slain, standing in the center of the throne, encircled by the four living creatures and the elders" (Rev. 5:6). If all our worship is not ultimately to him, for him, and about him, then all the shouting, singing, banging, and playing is just a lot of noise.

So worship is about a lifestyle. It's also about specific acts of devotion. And it's always to him, for him, and about him.

The Two-way Love Song

To finish this storyline, let's see what we discover by sneaking in on a few of the worship meetings that happened in the Bible.

In 1982, Mike was in his early twenties, and he remembers attending his first-ever conference, led by a bloke called John Wimber. Mike writes:

> I had heard about the great teaching, I was excited as I looked forward to the ministry, but it was in fact neither of these things that proved to be the highlight for me. Wimber's teaching was very good. It was at the same time biblical, deep, and very funny. The ministry was amazing—people were being empowered and healed all the way through the day. The thing that impacted me the most, however, was the worship. We sang simple

love songs to God one after the other, without pause. They may not have been the best tunes in the world, and some of the lyrics were far from Shakespearean, but the thing that both unhinged me and healed me was encountering the manifest presence of God as we sang. It really felt like coming home. God was really, really there, and he took my breath away.

At the beginning of one session, Wimber told us that we were going to worship for 30–40 minutes at the beginning of every meeting. If we didn't like the songs or the style of the music, or needed a shot of caffeine, he was very happy for us to go out and get a coffee during that time. He then said something that really struck me: "You see, we're not worshipping for you …" I was sure he was going to say that we were worshipping for God. Instead he said "… this worship is for me and for my team; I just can't teach, and we can't minister until we've first been in the presence of God, ministered to him, and allowed him to minister to us."

Mike and I are both convinced about the truth of this sentiment. Worship is a two-way love song. As we sing to him, he rejoices over us "with singing" (Zeph. 3:17). Throughout the Scriptures we see an inseparable link between worship and the presence of God. The link is this: Worship is a response to God's manifest presence; it also ushers us into his manifest presence.

Before we look at how this is true for Israel as a nation, let's look at how this is true for one man, King David. Reading the Psalms, many of which are David's cries to the Lord, we find this:

> *One thing I ask of the LORD, this is what I seek: that I may dwell in the house of the LORD all the days of my life, to gaze upon the beauty of the LORD and to seek him in his temple. For in the day of trouble he will keep me safe in his dwelling; he will hide me in the shelter of his tabernacle and set me high upon a rock. (Ps. 27:4–5)*

The one thing King David sought, when all else was stripped away, was the presence of God: to sit in the house of God, to gaze on the face of God, to hide in the shelter of God. These psalms were his worship to God; it was through these psalms that he made known his deepest longing.

David sang with joy: "Where can I go from your Spirit? Where can I flee from your presence? … If I rise on the wings of the dawn, if I settle on the far side of the sea, even there your hand will guide me, your right hand will hold me fast" (Ps. 139:7, 9–10).

God's presence with David was what gave him both strength and comfort: "Even though I walk through the valley of the shadow of death, I will fear no evil, for you are with me; your rod and your staff, they comfort me" (Ps. 23:4).

He encouraged others to "taste and see that the LORD is good; blessed is the man who takes refuge in him" (Ps. 34:8).

And it was being outside God's presence that was his great fear when David sinned by committing adultery. He cried out for mercy and begged God: "Do not cast me from your presence or take your Holy Spirit from me" (Ps. 51:11).

Other psalms in the great hymnbook of Israel reveal that worship as a cry for the presence of God was not unique to David. For example: "As the deer pants for streams of water, so my soul pants for you, O God. My soul thirsts for God, for the living God. When can I go and meet with God?" (Ps. 42:1–2).

The psalmist goes on to remember the days when he was in the procession in the temple and they worshipped in the presence of God. This image of the panting deer shouldn't be romanticized. It isn't of Bambi prancing in the woods; the image is of the scorching heat of the Middle East. When a deer is panting for water, its throat is aching with thirst; it is longing for that which gives it life, and without which it will certainly die. This is the image the psalmists use to describe their longing to meet with God.

> How lovely is your dwelling place, O LORD Almighty! My soul yearns, even faints, for the courts of the LORD; my heart and my flesh cry out for the living God…. Better is one day in your courts than a thousand elsewhere; I would rather be a doorkeeper in the house of my God than dwell in the tents of the wicked. (Ps. 84:1–2, 10)

Again the psalmist's very flesh and his very heart are crying out, yearning, fainting to be in the presence of God.

In the book of Psalms, we see clearly the words *presence, dwelling,* and *tabernacle* linked very closely to worship. A number of the psalms of praise were praise for his presence. Throughout the psalms we see the authors mourning at being away from his dwelling place and longing to be back there. There is nothing in these psalms to suggest his theoretical presence or his abstract dwelling. The language is language of encounter, of meeting with God. If you like, the language is language of experience.

This link between the worship and the presence can be traced throughout Israel's history as a nation. When Israel lived in the wilderness, before the tabernacle was made and dedicated, Moses used to pitch a tent outside the camp. It was called the Tent of Meeting. Whenever Moses went into the tent, the presence of the Lord would descend in the form of a cloud: "Whenever the people saw the pillar of cloud standing at the entrance to the tent, they all stood and worshiped, each at the entrance to his tent" (Ex. 33:10).

Years later, when the temple was dedicated, worship and God's presence were again inseparably linked. If we read the story in 2 Chronicles 5—7, what happens is this: The people worship, God's presence falls, the people worship some more, God's presence falls again, the people worship again!

It begins in 2 Chronicles 5:12–14:

> *All the Levites who were musicians—Asaph, Heman,*
> *Jeduthun and their sons and relatives—stood on the*
> *east side of the altar, dressed in fine linen and playing*
> *symbols, harps and lyres. They were accompanied by*
> *120 priests sounding trumpets. The trumpeters and*

singers joined in unison, as with one voice, to give praise and thanks to the LORD. Accompanied by trumpets, cymbals and other instruments, they raised their voices in praise to the LORD and sang: "He is good; his love endures forever." Then the temple of the LORD was filled with a cloud, and the priests could not perform their service because of the cloud, for the glory of the LORD filled the temple of God.

So Israel worshipped, and the glory of God fell. Then Solomon prayed, in front of the whole of Israel, a prayer of dedication and worship:

He stood on the platform and then knelt down before the whole assembly of Israel and spread out his hands toward heaven. He said: "O LORD, God of Israel, there is no God like you in heaven or on earth—you who keep your covenant of love with your servants who continue wholeheartedly in your way." (2 Chron. 6:13–14)

After Solomon had prayed this …

… fire came down from heaven and consumed the burnt offering and the sacrifices, and the glory of the LORD filled the temple. The priests could not enter the temple of the LORD because the glory of the LORD filled it. When all the Israelites saw the fire coming

down and the glory of the LORD above the temple,
they knelt on the pavement with their faces to the
ground, and they worshiped and gave thanks to the
LORD, saying, "He is good; his love endures forever."
(2 Chron. 7:1–3)

The presence of God fell again, and Israel worshipped again!

What this incredible scene clearly shows is that worship is a response to the glory of God. Indeed, there are few of us who would be able to stop ourselves from crying out praise should the weight of God's glory fall on us. What this amazing description also shows is that worship has a place in ushering in the presence of God. This is shown elsewhere in Israel's history.

We find it with Joshua and the battle of Jericho in Joshua 6. The Lord told Joshua that he had already delivered Jericho into his hands. Then he told him to march around the city every day for six days, with all the armed men. Seven priests were to march ahead, blowing rams' horns—a form of worship. Behind the priests was the ark of the covenant, the symbol and reality of God's presence. On the seventh day they were to march around Jericho seven times and all give a shout. We assume that rather than shouting "goal!" or "hole in one!" they were shouting their praises and cries of victory to God. The walls came down, just as God had said. Which came first—worship or the manifest presence of God? The chicken or the egg? The point is they were there together. The victory was won.

In 2 Chronicles 20 we read another amazing story of the Lord winning a battle. This time it was for Jehoshaphat and the people of

Judah. The Moabites and the Ammonites had ganged up on God's people, and the Lord said to them:

> *Do not be afraid or discouraged because of this vast army. For the battle is not yours, but God's.... You will not have to fight this battle. Take up your positions; stand firm and see the deliverance the* LORD *will give you ... Go out to face them tomorrow, and the* LORD *will be with you. (2 Chron. 20:15, 17)*

Jehoshaphat and all the people bowed down and worshipped God because of this promise. Then the next day:

> *Jehoshaphat appointed men to sing to the* LORD *and to praise him for the splendor of his holiness as they went out at the head of the army, saying: "Give thanks to the* LORD, *for his love endures forever." As they began to sing and praise, the* LORD *set ambushes against the men of Ammon and Moab and Mount Seir who were invading Judah, and they were defeated. (2 Chron. 20:21–22)*

Once again we see the two things happening at the same time. The Lord promised his presence, and Israel worshipped. Israel worshipped and God was with them.

Moving into the New Testament, we see the same thing happen in Acts 16. Paul and Silas were in the deepest dungeon of a prison in Philippi. Then, about midnight:

Paul and Silas were praying and singing hymns to
God, and the other prisoners were listening to them.
Suddenly there was such a violent earthquake that
the foundations of the prison were shaken. At once
all the prison doors flew open, and everybody's chains
came loose. (vv. 25–26)

These guys had just been stripped and "severely flogged." At midnight, when most of us would have been trying to get in contact with Amnesty International, they were worshipping. The power of God came, and a miracle happened. As a result the jailer and his entire family were converted. To repeat a point we made earlier in the book: The power is in the presence. Someone once asked John Wimber, "What's your technique for healing?" He replied, "There's no technique; it's the presence of God."

Some years ago Mike was in a prayer and worship meeting and found himself sitting next to a very elderly lady. They were singing Psalm 134, and everyone was clapping. As the song came to an end, everyone stopped clapping except the old lady. After a few moments she realized she was the only one and stopped as well.

She then told the crowd what had happened. She'd been suffering from severe arthritis for the past few years—she hadn't even been able to hold a coffee cup. She said, "I haven't clapped for years, and as I was worshipping Jesus, I forgot that I couldn't clap. Look," she said, waving her hands, "he healed me when I wasn't looking!" When we worship, we are distracted from ourselves as we gaze in wonder and love upon him. Worship is a place of healing. A well-known hymn by Helen Lemmel reads:

Turn your eyes upon Jesus,
Look full in his wonderful face,
And the things of earth will grow strangely dim
In the light of his glory and grace.[3]

In Acts 2 the disciples were praying in the upper room. On the day of Pentecost, the Holy Spirit came and filled them. They spilled out into the streets, declaring the wonders of God in many different languages—this is called worship. A crowd gathered. Then they preached and three thousand were converted. This is another example of the presence of God and the worship of God happening at the same time, and leading to a demonstration of the power of God.

Jesus told his disciples, "For where two or three come together in my name, there am I with them" (Matt. 18:20). He promised he would be present when we gather in his name, whether it is to pray or to worship. One translation of Psalm 22:3 reads, "[The Lord] inhabitest the praises of Israel" (KJV).

Worship is a response to the presence of God; it also ushers in the presence of God.

So, in the storyline of worship through the Bible, we discover many amazing things. God made us to worship him, but instead we chose to worship creation. The first commandment God gave to Israel was to love him. The way Israel was to love God was through sacrifice, a way of showing him that he was more important than creation. Israel messed this up by worshipping idols. Even when Israel was sacrificing to the Lord, she found it impossible to live a completely righteous life. Perfect worship demanded a perfect worshipper. Jesus came as that perfect worshipper. He lived a totally perfect life, which ended in the perfect sacrifice on the cross. So perfect was this sacrifice that it was made once for all! We do not have to sacrifice anything to make up for our sins.

God's command to love him still stands, however. Just as it was for Israel and Jesus, worship for us is to be a lifestyle; we are to be living sacrifices, living every day to love and glorify God. But (and this is what we have concentrated on in this chapter), the storyline of worship confirms that worship is also very much specific acts of devotion. More than anything these acts of devotion are linked to God's presence. They are a crying out and a longing for his presence, they are a response to his presence, and they prepare the ground for and usher in his presence!

Worship Storyline Paperchase:

What do we worship?
- Deuteronomy 4:15–19; Romans 1:21–23 (humanity worships creation over the Creator)

Israel's worship:
- Deuteronomy 6:5 (love God; worship as an expression of love)
- Leviticus (the worship instruction manual)
- Deuteronomy 31:16; Joshua 24:19–20 (problem of idolatry)

Jesus' worship:
- Matthew 26:36–46 (Jesus prays, abandoned by his friends)
- John 4:34; 5:30 (his whole life was perfect worship)

— Hebrews 10:12 (the one perfect sacrifice of his death)

Our worship:

- Romans 12:1 (our whole lives are to be worship)
- 2 Chronicles 7; Matthew 2:11; 28:17; Revelation 4—5 (worship can also be specific acts of devotion)
- Exodus 15:1–21; Psalm 81:1–2; 149:1–5 (worship through song!)
- Ephesians 5:18–20 (always give thanks)

The two-way love song:

- Zephaniah 3:17 (God sings over us)
- Psalms 27:4–5; 139:7–10; 23:4; 34:8; 51:11; 42:1–2; 84:1–2, 10 (the deepest longings of the psalmists)
- Exodus 33:10; 2 Chronicles 5—7; Joshua 5:13—6:27; 2 Chronicles 20:21–22; Acts 16:25–26; Acts 2; Matthew 18:20; Psalm 22:3 (worship and the presence of God are linked throughout the Bible)

Discussion Questions:

- In the light of this storyline, what do you understand the word *worship* to mean? What evidence can we draw upon—both from Scripture and the world around us—to illustrate this?
- Does worship change us? Why or why not?
- If worship is for God alone, the audience of One, what practical difference could that make to our lives and church services?

7

The Storylines Continue

We hope you have enjoyed this journey through just some of the great storylines of the Bible, and if you now have a hunger to know more and go deeper into God's Word, then this little book has done its job. There won't be any discussion questions at the end of this chapter; instead we'd like to challenge you to discover yet another storyline on your own. What is it that God is trying to show you in his Word? Prayerfully consider this, and then go! You may even draw up your own paperchase or discussion questions. Or perhaps you and a friend could do this together. If you aren't quite ready to write your own, start by just looking for storylines in your personal study, in sermons, in worship, or wherever you see God. But most importantly just spend some time meditating on what that storyline means for your relationship with God—that's what the Bible is all about.

It may be that as you draw to the end of this book, there are still other questions you're pondering, such as who wrote the Bible? Why are we sure it's accurate? How can I go about reading it for myself? To that end we have included an appendix at the back of this book: "The What, Why, and How of the Bible." You may find it helpful to explore a few of these questions for yourself. All of our understanding of the world is drawn from the Bible, so we need to be clear about why that is. This chapter may not answer all of the questions, but hopefully it will get you started.

One of the great needs today is for men and women who really know their God, who passionately love him, to be prepared to do great exploits with him and have adventures in his name. It is impossible to know him with any confidence without understanding his Book. He has revealed his character, his ways, and his will in the Bible. The Bible is his story. It is also our story. The words of the Bible are words of truth, words of grace, and words of life. They show us the way and feed us on the journey. That doesn't mean there aren't hard passages in the Bible, and some stories are not easy to understand. At the same time, that doesn't mean they can't be understood. We are convinced that to devote ourselves to searching and studying the Scriptures is one of the best things we can do with our lives.

A word of caution, though: Studying needs to be linked with obedience. There is no point reading the Bible if we are not prepared to do what it says. Often obedience to the teachings of the Bible helps us understand its truth better than the best commentaries around. At the same time we need to realize that we do not study on our own. Through the centuries men and women have unearthed great truths from God's Word. They have written these discoveries down for our benefit. We would do well to stand on their shoulders. Above all we have the Holy Spirit, through whom the Scripture was written, ready to speak to our hearts as well as our minds through the Word of God. As we read, we also pray and obey. The journey into God's Word is a journey that will last the whole of our lives. The more we know our God, the more we'll love him; the more we love him, the more we'll go for it and do amazing things with him.

The Bible tells us that before we were ever born God knew what we were going to cost him. He laid the foundations of his plans throughout the Old Testament, plans that can only be understood when we realize that Jesus shoots through the story like a ray of light. Jesus came to seal a new covenant with us, a mark of God's commitment to us. God will never break that covenant—he is never going to let you go. God is desperate to find a way that we can love and enjoy his holy presence. He's enabled us to live in him, and through his Spirit he dwells in us. We bow before him as holy God and as our mighty King. We have become agents of his wonderful kingdom, a kingdom of no more mourning, death, crying, or tears. Through his people God is going to expand his rule. It's a rule that depends not on the love of power but the power of love. It's through this love that God brought about his life-changing plan of salvation—something that happens to us the instant we accept it and yet sinks deeper into our lives every day that we receive it. And to all of this, because of who he is, our only response is worship. Not a worship that is forced or false, but worship as it was meant to be—joyful, burden sharing, honest, heartfelt, free, and loving. Worship that realizes the truth—the truth that we were made for a deep relationship of love with our God.

He is speaking to you today. He wants you to go deeper into his Word because that is the only sure way that you can go further and more effectively into his world. Know your God! Make him known!

Appendix A

The Bible in 20 Pages

If you've turned to this section before beginning the rest of the book, we can definitely sympathize. For those of us who've just become Christians, or for those of us who were experts at falling asleep during Sunday school, a reminder of the big picture, the grand narrative, is always helpful....

There are lots of stories in the Bible, but like *The Lord of the Rings,* they're all part of one big story. This story is HIS story. This story is also our story. But above all, this story tells of the relationship between God and humanity: the highs and the lows, the joys and the heartbreak, God's never-ending pursuit of a relationship with those he loves.

The first four words of the Bible are "In the beginning God." The Bible makes no attempt to explain what there was before God. It simply makes the point that everything begins with God. As we tell the story, then, let us begin at the beginning, with God....

The Creation Story

God created "something" out of nothing. We call it the universe. He created towering mountains, unfathomable oceans, spectacular waterfalls, and beautiful views.

He created dense forests, wide-open plains, and a world that bursts with variety from its animals to its insects, from its flowers to its fruits, and, as the centerpiece of his creation, he made something that would resemble him. That something was plural—it was Adam and Eve. Together, Adam and Eve reflected his image and likeness. It was only once he'd created Adam and Eve that he declared his creation to be "very good." Adam and Eve were created for relationship with and dependence on God. They were given the task of ruling (which means "looking after") the rest of creation on God's behalf. But instead of embracing this relationship, they messed it up. Choosing not to trust God, they opted for a life of independence.

The first course on the menu of independent life was forbidden fruit, and the side effects included loss of innocence and death. Adam and Eve, having eaten the fruit, lost their innocence, and when God came to hang out at the bottom of the garden, they realized for the first time that they were naked, and they hid from him.

The human race has been hiding from him ever since.

I (Andy) recently spent some time in India. While there I was sitting outside reading a book (in order to steal bits for this book). I glanced down and noticed a large ant, the type that has a nasty bite, moving threateningly in the direction of my foot. With one watchful eye on the ant, I turned to a friend and announced with feeling, "If that ant even thinks about biting me, I'm going to stamp on its head!" Wouldn't you do the same to an insect or wasp that stung you? It wasn't until a few minutes after I'd turned back to reading that I suddenly wondered—what if God had said that about us? "If the human race even thinks about hurting me, I'm going to stamp on them!"

The story of the Bible is different from this situation in two ways: First, the ant (in fact the whole colony of ants in the story—the human ants) did bite God; and second, God did not stamp. Why?

The Bible makes clear that God did not create us because he was lonely or bored. We're not there to satisfy his curiosity. Nor were we created in order to "complete him." The Christian doctrine of the Trinity implies many things, not the least of which is that God is a relational God. Father, Son, and Holy Spirit live for eternity in a perfect community of love. It was as if, one day in all eternity, the Father said to the Son and Holy Spirit: "We have so much love for each other, let's create something that looks like us, sounds like us, and smells like us—then we can share our love with it."

The first five days of creation were about God preparing the nursery. He chose the color scheme (mainly greens and blues); he ensured there were thousands of starry nightlights; and he laid down a carpet of meadows, deserts, and seas. Then on day six, humanity was born. We are told that out of the dust of the earth God created Adam, but there was no life in him.

Then God breathed his life into Adam.

Many of us might imagine it happened something like this: God was standing with his feet on Earth, his waist around Mars, and his head somewhere north of Jupiter. He took a big tube, placed one end strategically over Adam's nostrils, and blew. The whole of the Bible implies it happened differently. There wasn't a cosmic distance involved; it was as if God knelt down, lifted Adam's head slightly, and gave him the kiss of life.

When God made humanity, he was not constructing a car; he was having children. It was relational, it was intimate. "God said, 'Let *us* make man in our image, in our likeness …'" (Gen. 1:26). In other words it's as if the three persons of the Trinity were so full of love for each other, they couldn't help express it—they couldn't help but create something out of that love. God wasn't about to stamp on us, because we are so much more to him than a colony of biting insects. The view he has of us is so much higher and richer: We're his kids.

Something similar happens when boy meets girl. They fall in love and get married. In a perfect love story their love grows deeper each day. They are so in love they'd be happy to live, just the two of them, on a desert island for the rest of their lives. However, as with many married couples, the two decide that making something in their own image and in their own likeness will give new and wonderful expression to the love that already exists between them. So they have a child. They make something that looks like them, sounds like them, and, well, sometimes smells like them. This is called "the parenting instinct." It's an instinct we get from some-where, and it is God who has the original parenting gene.

Because we are his children, created in his image, God didn't flatten us when we walked out on him. With a click of his fingers, God could have wiped out creation and, if he'd wanted, started again. Instead of destroying everything, however, God chose not to give up on his children. The story of the Bible is God's plan of action—his plan to restore the relationship he'd always longed for with his children. As we read it, we're reading the story of God relentlessly pursuing us, not because he needs to, but because he rates us so highly that he longs to be in relationship with us.

Abraham (and Sons') Story

The plan to bring us back into that relationship kicks in with a guy called Abraham. Here's what God said to this wandering nomad:

> *Leave your country, your people and your father's household and go to the land I will show you. I will make you into a great nation and I will bless you; I will make your name great, and you will be a blessing. I will bless those who bless you, and whoever curses you I will curse; and all peoples on earth will be blessed through you. (Gen. 12:1–3)*

He then made an agreement, a covenant, with Abraham. This agreement was the basis and foundation on which his relationship with his people was to be built (see Chapter 2: The Covenant Storyline).

Skipping a few generations, Abraham had a son, Isaac, who had a son called Jacob (who later had his name changed to Israel). Jacob's favorite son was Joseph. Joseph's brothers were jealous and, as older brothers do, sold Joseph into slavery. Joseph ended up in Egypt and had a pretty rough time of it until miraculously he became prime minister. There was a famine in that whole region, but Joseph was warned by God through a dream and made sure the Egyptians had enough food. When his family came to Egypt begging for food, they discovered he was still alive and had done pretty well for himself! They were reunited, and the whole family moved to Egypt. Ten of the other sons of Jacob and Joseph's two sons gave their names to what became the twelve tribes of Israel (see the book of Genesis, chapters 37 to 50). During the next four hundred years, they bred like rabbits and became an ethnic minority.

A long time after Joseph died, the descendants of Abraham, Isaac, and Jacob were oppressed as slaves by the Egyptians (see the book of Exodus). In their misery they cried out to God. God remembered his covenant with Abraham and was faithful to it—the rescue operation began. He sent a guy called Moses, armed to the teeth with ten deadly plagues, and eventually the pharaoh of Egypt had no choice but to let the Israelites go. The Israelites began a journey from Egypt to the land that God had originally promised Abraham. A journey across the desert—which would have taken eight days if they'd walked in a straight line—took forty years!

Israel's Beginnings

Getting Israel out of Egypt was the easy bit for God; getting "Egypt" out of Israel took a lot longer. Despite the fact God had rescued them, the Israelites spent most of their time moaning, fighting with each other, and wishing at times they could be back in Egypt as slaves. They kept wishing for the old life, bad as it was, unable to realize the goodness of the life God had ahead of them. Moses had to put up with their constant whining, and perhaps the lowest point came when, not too far from the Promised Land (Ex. 19), Moses went up a mountain to talk with God. God gave him the laws by which he wanted his people to live (called the Ten Commandments). When Moses came down, carrying the Law—in which the first commandment was "You shall have no other gods before me" (Ex. 20:3)—he discovered the people of Israel had built a statue and were worshipping it instead of God!

He asked God to forgive them, but sadly this disrespect for God was to become the recurring theme throughout Israel's history.

Moses died in the desert, and Joshua, his assistant, took his place as both the representative of God and the leader of Israel. After their forty years in the desert, Joshua led the people into the land that God had originally promised to their ancestor Abraham (see the book of Joshua). God ordered Israel to totally drive out all the people who already lived in the land. These other tribes lived lives of immorality and did terrible things such as sacrificing babies to the idols they worshipped. God warned his people not to mix with these tribes as he knew they would end up copying their actions and turn to worshipping idols instead of him.

The Life of Israel

The book of Judges begins with the death of Joshua. Israel kept getting into trouble and breaking the agreement (covenant) they had made with God by worshipping other gods. As a result God allowed them to be conquered by their neighbors time and again. When things started to get really rough, Israel would repent and call out to God, and God would have mercy on his people.

He sent them leaders called judges. Sometimes these leaders led the people to freedom; other times they didn't do such a great job.

As time passed, Israel noticed all the tribes around them had human kings, and so they asked God for a king of their own (1 Sam. 8). God relented and let them have their way. Saul became king and messed it up. Then God chose a little shepherd boy living in an obscure town called Bethlehem to be king; his name was David (1 Sam.16). Even though he sometimes got it badly wrong, David loved God with all his heart. His reign and that of his son, Solomon, was the high point of Israel's history. They became a powerful nation. Under David and Solomon, a temple for the Lord was funded and built. It became the central place of worship for all Israel. David, in addition to being a shepherd, a warrior, and a king, was also a great poet and musician. Many of the songs he wrote became hit worship songs; they can be found in a book called the Psalms.

After the reign of Solomon, the kingdom of Israel split in two. The ten tribes living in the north became the northern kingdom and kept the name Israel. The two southern tribes, Benjamin and Judah, became the kingdom of Judah; their capital city was Jerusalem. The books of Kings and Chronicles tell the history of the kings of Israel and Judah. On the whole, despite one or two kings who followed the ways of David, most of them led their people to the worship of other gods, especially the idol Baal. A key clause in the covenant with God was broken, and once the people had broken their relationship with God, they broke their relationship with each other. They treated each other with cruelty and injustice.

As we read the story of Israel and their various rulers, we have to keep in mind the purpose behind it all. The God who longs for relationship with humanity chooses to get it by taking a particular people to himself. They are to have exclusive rights to him and he to them—a bit like husband and wife have exclusive rights to each other. This is the big story that overlays all the other stories we read throughout the Old Testament.

The Exile of Israel
Often, as Israel sinned and walked away from God, he would send messengers called prophets to encourage them to be faithful to

their side of the covenant. These prophets were sent to both Israel and Judah and included men like Elijah, Elisha, Amos, Micah, Hosea, and Isaiah. Despite their best efforts they were largely ignored. Having been shoved aside in favor of other gods, the Lord eventually, in an effort to win his beloved people back, sent them into exile. The kingdom of Israel was conquered (around 722 BC) and taken into exile by the Assyrians, who lived in what is now northern Iraq (2 Kings 17). Jerusalem and the southern kingdom of Judah were conquered in the years leading up to 586 BC. They were taken into exile by the Babylonians, who lived in what is now southern Iraq (2 Kings 25).

The destruction of Jerusalem began a long period of exile for God's people. The key prophets throughout this time were Jeremiah, Isaiah, and Ezekiel. Lamentations is a book written of the destruction of Jerusalem; the poems describe and grieve over the horrors that took place. Some of the people in exile wrote songs expressing their pain, like Psalm 137, which says, "By the rivers of Babylon we sat and wept when we remembered Zion [Jerusalem]" (v. 1).

The great tragedy of the exile is that the things that marked Israel as God's unique, beloved people were lost. Being conquered, losing their king, and going into exile meant that:

- The temple, the place where God himself lived among his people, was destroyed.
- The land, long ago promised to Abraham as his inheritance, was lost.
- The law, given to them as the distinctive people of God, was now difficult to obey in a land with foreign laws.

Returning from Exile

With Jerusalem conquered and people exiled, the unthinkable had happened. Almost all the outward evidence of Israel's status as God's people, all the signs of her unique, intimate relationship with God himself, had been removed. To both the other nations and the people of Israel themselves, "God's people" appeared to be very much alone.

At this time prophets came to Israel to comfort them and to declare that God had not forgotten them.

He would bring them back to their land and send a Messiah (anointed leader) to rescue them. The prophets brought promises of a new covenant that God would make with his people and that would be linked with the coming Messiah. One of the most striking of these prophecies can be found in Jeremiah 31:31–34.

The prophet Ezekiel described how God would raise up the king of Persia, Cyrus, to destroy Babylon. Eventually God did cause the Babylonian empire to crumble and through Cyrus brought his people home. The stories of Ezra and Nehemiah as well as the prophecies of people like Haggai and Zechariah tell us how the temple was rebuilt and Jerusalem repopulated. Even so, despite all they'd been through and all God had done for them, his people still refused to be faithful to him; they continued to worship other gods. God sent more prophets including Habakkuk, Zephaniah, and Malachi. Most of his people refused to listen to their cries. Then, after Malachi, whose writings make up the final book of the Old Testament, came four hundred years of silence; only the echoes of the promise of a new covenant remained.

The love story of the Old Testament is one of God's heartbreak. Not only do his children reject him, but the people whom he calls his own—whom he sets out to woo and to protect—reject him as well. On the surface we read of a rebellious people, flawed kings, crazy prophets, rich palaces, and fierce battles. Running beneath it all is the desire of a mighty God for a real and intimate relationship with his children.

What Happened after the Old Testament?

During the four hundred years after Malachi, though the people of Israel had returned to their land, they never gained lasting independence. They were ruled by various nations—the Persians, the Greeks, and the Syrians—until finally a brief spell (about one hundred years) of freedom under their own leaders was ended when the Romans captured Jerusalem in 63 BC.

During this time the hope that God would send a Messiah to free Israel from foreign occupation grew among many. There were divisions among the religious and political groups of the day. Each wanted to preserve Israel's identity, though they disagreed as to how. One group, the *Pharisees,* sought to preserve Israel's identity by strictly enforcing the Law of Moses. They invented more laws as safeguards against the original law being broken. Another group, known as the *Herodians,* included many of the leading priests along with King Herod and his sons. They believed compromise with Rome was the best way to preserve traditions. The *Zealots* were the freedom fighters of the day. This group wanted to overthrow the Romans by force of arms and envisioned a Messiah who would lead them into battle. The *Sadducees* wanted to retain power through the priestly system, while a fifth group, the *Essenes,* separated themselves, retreating into the desert to be holy on their own and wait for their Messiah to arrive.

Against this backdrop, about two thousand years after God promised Abraham "through your offspring all nations on earth will be blessed" (Gen. 22:18), Jesus was born.

Jesus' Life

The birth of Jesus in Matthew begins the story of the New Testament and the fulfilment of the new covenant promised by the prophets. It marks the arrival of God in a fresh and phenomenal way into the life of his people. Rather than sending them another prophet to call them back to himself, God came in person. It happened in a stinking stable in an obscure town called Bethlehem. The event passed virtually unnoticed by the world, with only some shepherds and a few foreigners turning up to welcome the King into his kingdom. The fact we know so little about Jesus' childhood shows how silently the Maker slipped into his creation.

The first sign that something was up came through a very strange man—with an interesting taste in food and fashion—yelling at the top of his voice the words of Isaiah, "Prepare the way for the Lord, make straight paths for him" (Matt. 3:3). His name was John; his nickname was "the Baptist." John's cries lit the fuse, and forty days after he baptized Jesus, something exploded. Jesus began his public ministry. He went all over Judea and Galilee, preaching the good news of the kingdom of God, healing the sick, casting out demons, performing many miraculous signs, confronting injustice and hypocrisy wherever he found it—and even raising the dead.

Wherever Jesus went, men and women followed, including twelve guys he had specifically chosen to be his apprentices; we know them as the twelve disciples. Controversy followed Jesus as well.

The more his popularity with the people grew, the more he became a threat to the various factions. The Pharisees, the Herodians, the Zealots, and the Essenes were all very confused; the Messiah was not meant to look like this! In contrast to the legalistic Pharisees, Jesus put people ahead of regulations. Unlike the compromising Herodians, Jesus refused to flex his political muscles. To the hot-headed Zealots, Jesus said, "Turn the other cheek." Against the views of the Essenes, who desired separation from an unholy world, Jesus went to parties with sinners and tax collectors. To add to all this, he appeared to be committing the greatest blasphemy: He claimed to be divine. Every Jew knew there was only one God, and this man claimed to be one and the same. As a result they wanted to kill him.

Jesus was betrayed by one of his disciples, Judas, and accused by the religious rulers. Sentenced by Pontius Pilate and nailed to the cross by Roman soldiers, he died on a Friday and two days later, to the surprise and joy of his followers, he rose from the dead. This is the central event of the story of the Bible; it is the pinnacle of God's plan of action to reunite himself with his people. We all know that real love costs us, and it's the same with God—ultimately it cost him his life. As we saw while exploring the storylines, the whole story of the Bible leads up to the death and resurrection of Jesus.

Over the next forty days Jesus appeared to many of his followers and gave them instructions. Just before he ascended into heaven, he appeared to the disciples and gave them what has become known as the Great Commission, saying, "All authority in heaven and on earth has been given to me. Therefore go and make disciples of all nations" (Matt. 28:18–19). To the same disciples he gave instructions to wait in Jerusalem for the gift of the Holy Spirit promised by his Father.

The Life of the Church

The disciples did what they were told. They waited. It was on the Jewish feast of Pentecost, when they were all together, that the breath of God came. Filled with the Spirit of God, they were suddenly empowered to do as Jesus had taught them. They set out to be witnesses and to continue the plan of renewed creation that began when God made his covenant with Abraham to bless all nations through him. On that day around three thousand people became Christians. Over the following years the church kept growing, continuing the ministry of Jesus. The book of Acts tells the story of how they proclaimed the good news of the kingdom of God, cared for the poor, planted many churches, and grew in numbers. Acts tells of how the followers of Christ, just like Jesus, healed the sick, cast out demons, performed many miraculous signs, confronted injustice and hypocrisy wherever they found it, and even raised the dead!

A short way through Acts we are introduced to Paul, who had been a zealous Pharisee and persecutor of the church until he met Jesus under rather unusual circumstances. He became one of the most significant leaders of the early church, spearheading the preaching of the news of Jesus to those who weren't Jewish, known as the Gentiles. He also wrote most of the letters, to both churches and individuals, found in the New Testament. Other letters are written by Peter, John, and a guy called James (probably Jesus' half-brother), and some (like Hebrews) are anonymous.

The End of the Story—It Hasn't Happened Yet!

The last book of the Bible, Revelation, is an account of prophetic visions that John, a disciple of Jesus, received while in exile on the island of Patmos. It has many strong links with Old Testament books, particularly Daniel and Ezekiel. It contains revelation of the glory of Jesus and the celebration going on in heaven as well as prophecy about the last days and the eventual return of Christ to earth (the second coming). Revelation is the book that looks forward to the completion of God's plan of action, the restoration of paradise, and the final ending of the pain, war, and disease that came with the sin of Adam and Eve. This is the picture of the ultimate fulfillment of everything God has been bringing about through the other sixty-five books of the Bible. It is at this point that we as the human race will finally be fully restored into that relationship of love with him. The amazing thing about the fact that the end hasn't been brought about yet is that it means we are living *in* the story. We worship and have a relationship with the God of this story. It is his story, but it is also our story. It's the story of that relationship.

That's a whistle-stop tour of the Bible! The table below might also be helpful for getting the overview. And now that we've familiarized ourselves with a grand overview of the love story of Scripture, we can turn back to chapter 1 and begin to explore the first storyline—Jesus. Mike and I are so excited about everything we've discovered whilst studying and reading for this book. Decades of Sunday school meant we kind of knew bits of the big story, but what's amazed us has been looking at it from different angles. As we mentioned in our introduction, picking the storylines of Scripture apart and then weaving them back together leaves us so much more able to appreciate the richness, the depth, and the glory of the Bible's story and the Bible's God. We invite you to come on that journey with us.

Book	Description
The Pentateuch: Genesis Exodus Leviticus Numbers Deuteronomy	The first five books of the Bible are known as the Pentateuch. They tell the story of the creation of the world (*Genesis* means "beginning") and the rebellion of the human race. They speak of God forming a people (called Israel, and later called the Jews) with whom he could have a relationship. Here we read the critical story of God saving Israel from Egypt and taking them on an "exodus" from Egypt to the Promised Land. The Pentateuch also contains the Law that God gave Moses for the people to follow. These laws include moral laws, ceremonial laws, and dietary laws.
History Books: Joshua Judges Ruth 1 Samuel 2 Samuel 1 Kings 2 Kings 1 Chronicles 2 Chronicles Ezra Nehemiah Esther	These books are the history books. They tell the history of Israel from the time they entered the Promised Land. They describe how Israel conquered the land and established a kingdom. They tell of the adventures of Israel's leaders (the most famous being King David), both their successes and their failures. They describe how Israel turned from God and how the kingdom of Israel split in two. The history books tell us of Israel repeatedly rejecting God, being conquered, going into exile and then eventually returning from exile.

Poetry Books:	These are the poetry books, or wisdom literature. Proverbs includes many of Israel's wise sayings. The Psalms are Israel's worship songs to God. Job is one of the earliest attempts to understand the problem of suffering. Ecclesiastes needs to be read with antidepressants (if you don't believe us, check it out). There is even a rather raunchy love poem—see Song of Songs.
Job Psalms Proverbs Ecclesiastes Song of Songs	
Major Prophets:	These are the prophetic books. The reason some prophets are called "major" and others "minor" is because some have bigger books than others. God sent Israel prophets throughout her history. Before the exile (at the end of 2 Kings), God sent the prophets to warn Israel of what was about to happen and to encourage her to turn back to God. During the exile the prophets came to Israel to explain why the exile had happened and to speak hope and forgiveness over her. They promised a restoration of Israel would take place and hinted at a ruler being sent by God to save Israel. After the return from exile, God sent yet more prophets to encourage his people not to turn away from him. These prophets, whose voices make up the last books of the Old Testament, also speak of a future hope...
Isaiah Jeremiah Lamentations Ezekiel Daniel	
Minor Prophets:	
Hosea, Joel, Amos, Obadiah, Jonah, Micah, Nahum, Habakkuk, Zephaniah, Haggai, Zechariah, Malachi	

400 years of silence
A series of books known as the Apocrypha was written during this time. See Appendix B, "The What, Why, and How of the Bible," for further discussion.

History Books:	The first four, Matthew to John, are the Gospels (literally the "good news") about Jesus. They tell the story of the birth, life, death, and resurrection of Jesus. Each gospel tells the story from a slightly different perspective. In Acts, Luke tells the history of the early church.
Matthew Mark Luke John Acts	
Letters:	
Romans, 1 Corinthians, 2 Corinthians, Galatians, Ephesians, Philippians, Colossians, 1 Thessalonians, 2 Thessalonians, 1 Timothy, 2 Timothy, Titus, Philemon, Hebrews, James, 1 Peter, 2 Peter, 1 John, 2 John, 3 John, Jude	These letters were written to churches and individuals. Paul is traditionally considered the writer of the letters from Romans to Philemon. Various others wrote Hebrews to Jude. Many of the letters were written to correct bad teaching or to address sinful practices. They were also written to give hope and encouragement to early Christians.

Prophecy:	This is one of the trickiest books of the Bible to understand. There are prophetic elements to it, and it has strong links to the Old Testament prophecies of Daniel and Ezekiel. It was also written to bring encouragement to a church, which by then was being persecuted.
Revelation	

Appendix B

The What, Why, and How of the Bible

Having looked at some of the great themes of Scripture, we now want to turn to look at the Bible itself: how it came to be written, the claims it makes about itself, and why certain books are included and others excluded. Then there are some suggestions on how best to read the Bible for yourself.

Sometimes the Bible is used as a good luck charm or as a religious version of the national lottery—"open up the book randomly and see if your numbers come up." This can lead to very strange results. Someone once prayed, "Lord, speak to me, guide me through your Word." He then opened up the Bible and put his finger down on a verse. It said, "[Judas] went away and hanged himself" (Matt. 27:5). Our friend thought he'd try again. The next random scripture was, "Go and do likewise" (Luke 10:37). Probably not the best way to get guidance. Sometimes we can read bits of the Bible totally out of the context of the verses around them. This is a little like eating the pickle in a cheese-and-pickle sandwich and leaving everything else. We have heard of one woman who drives into the center of her town always full of faith that she will find a parking space in the perfect location, for after all, Jesus said in John 14:3, "I go and prepare a place for you." Others seem to use the Bible as a weapon with which to beat up fellow Christians and resort to proof texts that they hurl as hand grenades at the opposition....

So what is the Bible, and how should it be used?

How Did the Bible Become the Bible?

The word *Bible* is related to the Greek meaning "book" or "library," and, as we noted in the introduction, the Bible is a library of sixty-six books or pieces of writing. The Bible didn't come into existence through God writing the whole thing up in heaven, dictating it to the angel Gabriel and signing a deal with King James for its publication on earth. The sixty-six books were written by many different people, at many different times, in many different places, and with many different objectives. None of these people had any idea their work was going to end up gathered together into the one Book, and yet, amazingly, as we have discovered through our tracing of the storylines, this collection of sixty-six books tells one incredible, coherent, intentioned, purposed story. This was no accident ... but how did the Bible come to be?

We believe the Bible is the inspired Word of God and therefore is the ultimate authority for followers of Jesus in all matters of faith and lifestyle. At the same time, the Bible contains the words of lots of different human beings who were writing their thoughts, beliefs, and opinions, and were putting down their memory of events. These human beings were imperfect, sinful, and limited in their understanding. Nevertheless God uses the collection of their words to reveal who he is, who we are, how we relate to him, and how we relate to each other. The collection of these words is his Word, his message, his revelation to us.

Once we've acknowledged that the Bible both is written by humans and is God's Word, questions immediately arise about when, how, and why these writings were collected together and the decision made that they were to be part of the "Bible."

The Bible is referred to as "the canon of Scripture." This isn't the type of cannon you'd find on a pirate ship; canon in this context means a measuring rod, something that marks out the boundaries of what's in and what's out. So when we refer to the canon of Scripture, we're talking about the writings we view as the inspired Word of God; they are the ones that made the cut. Books not in the canon are not believed to have divine authority.

When certain books came to be seen as having God-given authority is a historically tricky subject to grapple with—not least because they were written at different times! The books that Christians refer to as the Old Testament were written and edited by different Jewish writers over about a thousand years. It would be an oversimplification to believe that, by the time of Jesus, people were able to go to the temple bookshop and buy a nice leather-bound copy of the Old Testament. However, certainly by this time there was an established body of writing that was regarded as having God-given authority. Jesus himself, along with Paul, Peter, and others, quoted many and varied passages from the Old Testament and they certainly saw it as having divine authority. While no doubt the opponents of Jesus and his followers disagreed with their interpretation of Scripture, Jesus never had an argument with the Pharisees about what was or was not Scripture. It is very clear that the early Christians regarded the books we now know as the Old Testament as holy Scripture—the New Testament had yet to be written.

At this point it is perhaps worth discussing a collection of books known as the Apocrypha. Some Bibles, particularly those belonging to Catholics, include these books in addition to the Old Testament. Where did they come from and why do many Bibles not include them?

Again, these books were written over a long period of time, but the majority of them came into being during the four-hundred-year gap between the end of Malachi and the beginning of the New Testament. Just as we have our NIV, NRSV, and other translations of the Bible, much of the Mediterranean world around this time used a translation of the Old Testament called the Septuagint. *Septuagint* just means "seventy" and comes from the tradition that seventy scholars translated the Old Testament (written in Hebrew) into Greek (which most of the Mediterranean world spoke). Some of the Apocryphal books are included with the Old Testament books in the Septuagint (translated around 285 to 246 BC). Though many Christians for several hundred years after Jesus would have read the Septuagint, the little evidence we have about an early Old Testament canon seems to indicate the Apocrypha was not regarded as having the same level of authority as the rest of the Old Testament.

The Jewish historian Josephus, who lived during the first century, lists the canon of the Old Testament without including the Apocryphal books, and we have a record of a group of Jewish scholars getting together in AD 90 to discuss the Old Testament canon—again not including the Apocryphal books. The early Christians did not regard these books as having the same divine weight as the rest of the Old Testament.

They were first grouped together into the whole Bible (Old and New Testaments) by a guy called Jerome around AD 400, but he himself tells us that this was because he saw them as "helpful," not because he thought they were divinely inspired. After Jerome it became common to include the Apocrypha with the Old Testament until the 1500s. During a period called the Reformation, the church in the West divided into Protestants and Catholics, and the Protestants removed the Apocryphal books from the Old Testament. The Roman Catholic Church, however, decided to officially include the Apocrypha in its canon. That's why you'll find some Bibles with and some Bibles without these extra books in the Old Testament. While we personally don't believe the Apocrypha should be part of the canon of Scripture, it is important to note that even if it is included (as is the case for many of our Catholic friends), this doesn't alter any of the core teachings of the church.

It is very difficult to accurately date some of the books of the New Testament, but most of them seem to have been written between AD 45 and AD 140. However, it wasn't until the Council of Hippo in AD 393 and the Council of Carthage in AD 397 that the bulk of the church finally agreed on the thirty-nine books of the Old Testament and the twenty-seven books of the New Testament as the canon. At these councils a group of bishops got together and decided what should be in and what should be out. How do we account for the hundreds of years between the date of these finished writings and the decision to include them as Scripture? Should it really take that long to decide whether or not they were divinely inspired?

Well, all the evidence indicates that Christians saw the books we now know as the New Testament as having this God-given authority much earlier than the councils. Support for this comes from the fact that the New Testament writings were translated into many different languages at a very early stage and spread throughout the Mediterranean (implying they were seen as having some authority). We also know that in many of the earliest Christian services the writings of the apostles would be read aloud. None of this would have happened were it not for the fact that these writings were already being seen as having divine authority.

Loads of the theology of the early church was written by people who are now collectively called "the church fathers." Many of them quoted from the New Testament, citing it as having binding authority. One of these theologians, Justin Martyr, who lived AD 110–165, would use the significant phrase "it is written," and go on to quote from the Gospels. Other church fathers—for example Origen and Eusebius in the second and third centuries—listed books they saw as authoritative, and these lists largely correspond to what we now know as the New Testament. Some books eventually included in the canon were more contested than others, but these debates were not, as *The Da Vinci Code* would have us believe, whispered conspiracies behind closed doors. They were openly debated, and the eventual decision to include them was not a snap decision by a small group of people but the natural consensus, over time, by the majority of the church. By the time the councils came along in AD 393 and 397, they did little more than confirm a New Testament canon that the majority of the church had already accepted as divinely inspired for years.

In that case we might ask why the councils were even needed. The reason was that by this point the church had grown enormously and spread to many different countries and cultures. What's more, the first apostles of the church had died hundreds of years before. All this meant that there were disagreements arising as to what the church's official teaching was. Certain groups of believers were taking a radically different stance from the original teachings of Jesus and the apostles. The councils were aimed at ending these disagreements. They "closed the canon." Closing the canon meant that they formally recognized which books were divinely inspired and which were not. This meant that, as the church spread and time passed, other writings could not be added to the Scriptures.

As Christians we believe that the Bible is the Word of God, God-breathed and divinely inspired. At the same time, we believe that just as God chose to work through human beings in the Bible, he chose to work through human beings in writing the Bible. We also believe he chose to work through human beings as they sought to recognize divinely inspired Scripture. There is no neat and tidy formula as to how the canon came to be, but as the Holy Spirit guided those in the Bible, so too he guided the church as, over time, in an organic way, certain writings came to be recognized and set apart as divinely inspired.

How Do We View the Bible?

Whether or not we're still at school, all of us have had days when we've arrived and the teacher has been off sick. They may have left a note on the whiteboard with instructions for the lesson. Would we have quietly settled down and done the exercise set? More often than not it would depend on the teacher. If they were one of those teach-ers who had no control, even when they were in the classroom, then probably not. If they were one of those teachers who had to scream, shout, and lose their temper every five minutes, then probably not. If they were one of those teachers who tried to act cool and like one of us, when they obviously weren't, then probably not. If they were one of those teachers who tried to bribe the class with food and promises of films, then probably not. If they were the kind of teacher where the whole class could get away with humming loudly under their breath (while the teacher was reduced to tears trying to detect the source of the humming), probably not.

On the other hand, if the note on the whiteboard had been left by one of those teachers who, without raising her voice or getting up from her desk, could silence the room with a single word, one of those teachers you couldn't help but respect, we probably would have followed the instructions on the whiteboard.

All of us know that in this scenario, those teachers who had little authority were likely to have had far fewer exercises to mark the next day than those who had lots of authority. The writing on the white-board, by itself, had no authority—it was the authority of the teacher acting through the writing that made the difference.

It's similar when it comes to the Bible. When we speak of the "authority of the Bible," we are really speaking of the authority of God working through the Bible. In Matthew 28:18, Jesus declares, "All authority in heaven and on earth has been given to me." When the wind and waves on the Sea of Galilee started kicking up a fuss, Jesus simply said, "Be still," and they obeyed. Our guess is that if a whole classroom of us all started humming under our breath and

Jesus, without looking up from his desk or raising his voice, asked us to be still, we would. Forget the classroom, all the authority in the universe belongs to him! The point here is not that God is like an absent school teacher and the Bible a list of exercises; it is that we regard the Bible as the ultimate authority because of the fact that God himself chooses to exercise his authority through it.

What Does the Bible Say about the Bible?

As we've already mentioned, Jesus quoted the Old Testament all the time. He began his ministry by reading from the prophet Isaiah and saying, "Today this scripture is fulfilled in your hearing" (Luke 4:21). In his time in the wilderness, Jesus responded to all three of the Devil's temptations by quoting Scripture. Elsewhere he said of the Old Testament Law that "not the smallest letter, not the least stroke of a pen, will by any means disappear from the Law until everything is accomplished" (Matt. 5:18). In his anger, cleansing the temple, he quoted from Isaiah and Jeremiah (Luke 19:46). Speaking to the people about himself, he quoted Psalm 118:22 (Luke 20:17). There are many other examples, but what is clear is that Jesus both knew the Old Testament scriptures and regarded them as the words of God.

In his second letter Peter refers to Paul's letters as a little difficult to understand and that "which ignorant and unstable people distort, as they do the other Scriptures" (2 Peter 3:16). The clear implication of this is that Peter regarded at least some of Paul's letters as Scripture.

Paul also often referred to Old Testament scriptures, and in 2 Timothy 3:16–17 he says, "All Scripture is God-breathed and is useful for teaching, rebuking, correcting and training in righteousness, so that the man of God may be thoroughly equipped for every good work." For Paul to say all Scripture is God-breathed is another way of saying it is divinely inspired. When Paul says to Timothy that it is useful for teaching, rebuking, and so on, he is saying, in other words, "Know this Book—it is the practical guide to the Christian life!"

What's more, the authority that the Bible has stems from its purpose in God's plan. God's aim, as we have discovered again and again in this book, is not that we complete certain exercises but that we grow in relationship with him. It is for this reason that the Bible points beyond itself back to God. Reading the Bible should never stop with the writing on the page; the Bible is drawing us closer and pushing us further toward God himself. Our hope as you delve deeper into the Bible is not so much that you would think, "Wow! Isn't the Bible an amazing book?" but more that you would think, "Wow! Isn't God an amazing God?" The Bible does not primarily point beyond itself toward things to do; it points beyond itself toward a God who is love.

Jesus once told the Pharisees off by saying, "You diligently study the Scriptures because you think that by them you possess eternal life. These are the Scriptures that testify about me, yet you refuse to come to me to have life" (John 5:39–40). N. T. Wright has pointed out that "when John declares that 'in the beginning was the word,' he does not reach a climax with 'and the word was written down' but 'and the word became flesh.'"[4] The climax of reading the Bible for Christians shouldn't be growing in our knowledge of the words on a page but growing in our knowledge of the Word made flesh … and it's so much more exciting that way!

The Bible is the ultimate authority for Christians in faith and lifestyle because God, who has all authority, chooses to exercise his authority through it. The authority the Bible has comes from its role in God's plan (God's plan is for a relationship of mutual love), and so God exercises his authority through the Bible as it serves to draw us into this relationship with him.

How Do We Read It?

So how do we read the Bible? First of all, prayerfully. If we believe that the Bible was written by the Holy Spirit, then clearly he who inspired the Bible is the best interpreter of it. So before reading God's Word it's always good to ask the Holy Spirit to reveal the truths of it to us. This in no way suggests that we leave our brains at the door, but it does mean we choose to come to the Bible in humility, with an attitude less of us examining and dissecting it, and more of it examining and dissecting us: "For the word of God is living and active. Sharper than any double-edged sword, it penetrates even to dividing soul and spirit, joints and marrow; it judges the thoughts and attitudes of the heart" (Heb. 4:12).

There are many different ways we can read the Bible. Sometimes it's helpful to read it as a novel, and this way we get the big picture. It's like wandering into an art gallery and looking at one of those scenic paintings. To read the Bible as a novel is to take in the whole of the artist's canvas. It is to drink in the lie of the land and the beauty of the finished work. But then, in order to appreciate the painting more, you have to look more closely and inspect. Often at this point it's useful to have an expert helping—someone who can point out the different shades, the way the colors blend into each other, the way the artist has painted so as to draw the eye here or there. Now is the time to pay attention to detail. So it is with reading God's Word;

having taken in the big picture, we now take our magnifying glass and study carefully particular books, passages, or themes. It's often very helpful to learn from those who have studied before us—Bible teachers and writers of commentaries and study guides.

Let's look at a few practical examples:

Verse-by-verse Studies

For example, take one of the letters. Read it through verse by verse, line by line, asking questions: "Who was the letter written to?" "What was the purpose of the letter?" "What questions was the letter trying to answer?" "What was the historical context the letter was written in?" In other words we are trying to read the white spaces between the sentences in order to understand the sentences. Reading commentaries and study aids written by biblical historians who have looked into this helps us to answer these questions. The basic question we're trying to answer here is, "What did it mean?" Only when we have some answer to this question can we begin to answer the second, very practical question, "What does it mean?" In other words, "What is the application for my life today?" Sometimes, if we don't attempt to answer the first question, we can misread the Scripture and come up with some very bizarre answers to the second question.

Character Studies

This is another great way of studying Scripture. To look, for example, at the life of Joseph and ask what lessons you can learn. Joseph has dreams as a young man, and he seems to boast about these dreams. He is then sold into slavery, unjustly accused of rape, imprisoned, and forgotten for years. Eventually he is released. His gift with dreams is used and he prospers. His original dream is fulfilled when his brothers come and bow before him, but God has worked humility into him through the years of suffering, and instead of boasting he weeps. Three of the great lessons from the life of Joseph are:

1. Don't give up on your dreams and gifting.
2. God uses suffering to prepare us for success, so that when it comes it won't ruin us.
3. God is sovereign; he is in charge even when it doesn't feel like that.

So by doing a character study through the Bible, the lives of these people can speak profoundly into our lives today.

Themes

A third way to study Scripture is to look at themes that run all the way through. This is largely the approach we have taken in this book. It can even take the form of a word study. For example: *glory, kingship, faith,* or *joy.*

Meditation

If you learned about an artist's reason for painting, studied the way he created it, and looked at it with your magnifying glass, it would also be important to simply stand and enjoy it. Or you may look at one part of the painting and allow it to speak to you. Meditation is similar to this idea. Christian meditation on the Bible has a long history but is undervalued today. Sometimes in our culture, where everything has a purpose and meaning, we can forget to enjoy the beauty of God's Word and forget to allow it to bring joy to our souls as well as inform our minds. Practically this can mean simply taking one verse or one line and gazing at it for days and allowing it to speak to us. An example could be the first line of Psalm 23. This line can be read at least five different ways. First meditate for a few minutes on this: "THE Lord is my shepherd." Then, "The LORD is my shepherd." Then, "The Lord IS my shepherd." Then, "The Lord is MY shepherd." Finally, "The Lord is my SHEPHERD." If you've spent time on this, you will have mined depths to this one line that we never would have thought were there simply by reading it and moving on.

So there are plenty of ways we can enjoy reading the Bible; we have suggested: as a novel, through verse-by-verse study, through character studies, through looking at themes, and through meditation. It's really good for us to take all these approaches at different times—it's like having a healthy and balanced diet. If we are to get the best out of God's Word (or God's Word is to get the best out of us), then approaching the Bible in different ways is essential.

Helpful Principles for Tough Passages

We all know that there are some passages in the Bible that are really difficult to make sense of. Two principles that are helpful for interpreting tough passages are interpreting Scripture with Scripture and reading through the lens of Jesus.

1. Interpreting Scripture with Scripture

The first principle that helps us to understand difficult passages is that Scripture should always be interpreted by Scripture. This is one of the reasons we need to have a balanced diet. To have a purely narrow reading of the Bible means it can be easy to take verses out of context. For example, you could add up all the scriptures that talk about prosperity, wholeness, health, and abundance, and come to the conclusion that there are so many references that it must always be God's will for us to be healthy, wealthy, and happy. We could also take the hundreds of scriptures that talk about poverty, having nothing, and giving up our possessions, and think, just by looking at them in isolation, that God's will for us is always to have nothing and to live without any material wealth.

It is only by interpreting Scripture with Scripture that we come to a balanced view of such things. Only such a reading leads us to Paul's summary in his letter to the Philippians:

> For I have learned to be content whatever the circumstances. I know what it is to be in need, and I know what it is to have plenty. I have learned the secret of being content in any and every situation, whether well fed or hungry, whether living in plenty or in want. I can do everything through him who gives me strength. (4:11–13)

2. Reading through the lens of Jesus

We can also gain a better understanding of difficult passages by knowing that Jesus is the lens through which we read the Bible. So when we read passages in the Old Testament about people being stoned, we must read them through the lens of Jesus' words in John 8:1–11, where a group of men is about to stone an adulteress to death: "If any one of you is without sin, let him be the first to throw a stone at her" (v. 7). We have already noted that Jesus announced that the Scriptures point to him. It is Jesus who makes sense of many scriptures. Isaiah 53 is very puzzling until we see Jesus' death on the cross. This is not to say Jesus is the gloss we use to cover up all the passages we don't like; it is, however, a very helpful principle when trying to understand how the Bible fits together. He is the place where the Bible comes together.

In this section we haven't tried to explain the difficult passages or answer all of the questions—loads of other books do this much better. But we do hope that you will find this Appendix helpful in providing guidelines as you delve deeper into the treasures and truths of the Bible, as you let it feed you, as you savor it, as you let it challenge you, as you let it change you, and as you let it speak its message of hope, joy, and love into your life.

Notes

1. Matt Redman, "Lord Let Your Glory Fall," © 1998 Thankyou Music (www.worshiptogether.com and www.kingswaysongs.com), 2004 EMI. Used by permission of Thankyou Music.
2. Martyn Layzell, "Lost in Wonder," © 2002 Thankyou Music (www.worshiptogether.com and www.kingswaysongs.com), 2006 EMI. Used by permission of Thankyou Music.
3. Helen Lemmel, "Turn Your Eyes Upon Jesus," public domain.
4. N. T. Wright, *The Last Word* (New York: HarperOne, 2005), 23.